Cornell University

Ithaca, New York

CORNELL STUDIES

IN

CLASSICAL PHILOLOGY

EDITED BY

BENJAMIN IDE WHEELER, CHARLES EDWIN BENNETT,
GEORGE PRENTICE BRISTOL, AND
ALFRED EMERSON

No. III

THE CULT OF ASKLEPIOS

BY ALICE WALTON PH.D.

PUBLISHED FOR THE UNIVERSITY
BY
GINN & COMPANY
1894

THE

CULT OF ASKLEPIOS

BY

ALICE WALTON, Ph.D.

Cornell Studies in Classical Philology, No. III

The Athenæum Press
GINN & COMPANY, BOSTON, U.S.A.

PREFACE.

IN writing upon a subject so familiar to the student of Greek life as the Cult of Asklepios, it is difficult to avoid following in the lines of work already done. Most of the material upon which the following pages are based has been worked over and over. The results of the excavations in the Athenian Asklepieion are well-known, and the Epidaurian steles are no longer recent discoveries. If the results of investigation are practically those of previous research, the excuse for re-working old material may be found in the method of their arrangement. Upon single features of the ritual of Asklepios much has been written in German, in French, and in English ; but no one has as yet attempted a general descriptive treatment of the cult as a whole. The facts are stated by Thraemer in the article " Asklepios " in Roscher's Lexicon of Greek and Roman Mythology in suggestive rather than narrative form, while Girard's work is complete only for the cult in Athens. It has been my aim to give in narrative form the results obtained by a careful comparison of material from the different localities, and also to show by means of indexes what material is used. The treatment is of necessity brief, as the work is not a series of monographs. The arrangement is topical, and so far as possible chronological. At the end of the narrative are two indexes, one of allusions to Asklepios and his cult in Greek and Latin literature and inscriptions, and the second is a classification of the localities in which the cult is known or supposed to have existed. The indexes overlap in many instances, and it cannot be claimed that they contain all the material which might have been used. The aim has been to make them exhaustive so far as concerns the inscriptions and important authors. The monumentary evidence has been used freely in the body of the work, but there is no attempt at a systematic collection of this material, as it was felt that it is a task for the student of art rather than of literature. There is added an index of topics and names which refers both to the discussion and the main indexes.

In the spelling of proper nouns, the Greek form is used, except in the cases of such as are thoroughly and familiarly anglicized.

I take this opportunity of expressing my hearty thanks to Dr. Benjamin Ide Wheeler of Cornell University for his kindly interest and advice during the preparation of the work, and to Professor Theodor Schreiber of Leipzig, who has critically read the manuscript and offered many valuable suggestions.

LEIPZIG, June, 1893.

CONTENTS.

—◆◆—

THE CULT OF ASKLEPIOS.

CHAPTER I.

ASKLEPIOS AS KNOWN TO HOMER.

In Homer, Apollo and not Asklepios is the god of health, though only so far as to send or abate pestilences. The divine physician is Paian, the attendant of the gods, who heals Hades[1] and Ares.[2] In the Odyssey every physician is said to be of the race of Paian,[3] which Aristarchus explains by saying that the physician's art is from Apollo, but his descent from Paian. Hesiod makes a distinction between the two.[4] Paian is occasionally mentioned later than Homer, but the name is used as an epithet of Apollo or of other deities who are connected with healing, as Asklepios and Athena, and then by an extension of meaning from "healer" to "savior," it was applied to Dionysos[5] and Thanatos[6] and occasionally even to men.[7] The forms of the word are variants of Παιάν, which Hesychius explains as a hymn sung to Apollo to avert a pestilence. Hence the use of the word as a form of address to Apollo and Asklepios.[8]

---

[1] E 401. Παιήων παρὰ τὸ παύειν τὰς ἀνίας, ὅ ἐστιν ὀδύνας. Sch. E 401.

[2] E 900.

[3] δ 232.

[4] διαφέρει ὁ Παιήων Ἀπόλλωνος ὡς καὶ Ἡσίοδος μαρτυρεῖ· εἰ μὴ Ἀπόλλων Φοῖβος ὑπὲκ θανάτοιο σαώσει, ἢ αὐτὸς Παιών, ὃς πάντα τε φάρμακα οἶδεν. Sch. δ. 232, Hes. ed. Marckscheffel, Frag. CCXX.

[5] Orph. Hymn. 52, 11.

[6] Eurip. Hipp. 1373; Aeschyl. Frag. 105.

[7] Plut. Lys. 18.

[8] Aristid. ed. Dindorf, 514, 17. Examples of the use of παιάν as an epithet are frequent; Ἀπόλλων II., Selinuntian inscription, Collitz, 3047; Oropos, Paus. I.

Asklepios is mentioned in the Iliad three times, but nowhere in the Odyssey. He appears only as the father of Machaon and Podaleirios, and twice is called the "blameless physician."

"The two sons of Asklepios led them, goodly physicians, Machaon and Podaleirios." [1]

"Call Machaon hither, the son of Asklepios, the blameless physician." [2]

"Machaon went beside, the son of Asklepios, the blameless physician." [3]

In the Catalogue, the Asklepiadæ led the forces from Trikka, Ithome and Oichalia, the first two of which lay in western Thessaly. This points to that region as the seat of the Asklepios cult, if indeed such a cult was in existence in the Homeric age. For Homer did not recognize the worship of Asklepios, but regarded him as one who like Achilles and Jason had learned his art from Chiron.[4] The connection with Chiron again localizes the cult, for the centaur legends come from Thessaly. A family of Chironidæ, famous for a secret knowl-

---

34, 3; Egypt, Rev. Arch. 1889, p. 71. Π. Ἀσκληπιόϛ, CIG. 511; CIA. III. 1; Add. et Corr. 171 a and b. Ἀθηνᾶ II., Paus. I. 34, 3. Theocritus applies the term to Apollo, V. 79; VI. 27; Ep. I. 3. The form Παιήων is used for the father of Asklepios: ἦλθε καὶ ἐς Μίλητον ὁ τοῦ Παιήονος υἱός. Ep. VII. 1. Welcker (Götterl. I. p. 695) tried to prove the existence of Paian as a god in post-Homeric times, on the ground that Cicero mentioned his statue in a temple of Aesculapius in Agrigentum. *Quid, signum Paeanis ex aede Aesculapii praeclare factum, sacrum ac religiosum, non sustulisti?* Cic. Verr. IV. 57. This, however, is no proof, for Paian is a frequent epithet of Apollo as a healing god, and particularly when brought into connection with Asklepios, as here. A coin of Agrigentum, on which a serpent is represented crawling over the face of Apollo, gives more striking evidence for the close relation of the two divinities, Apollo and Asklepios. Head, Hist. Num. 108. The Latin adjective *Paeonius* has a stereotyped meaning of "medicinal," and does not carry a ritualistic meaning.

[1] τὼν αὖθ' ἡγείσθην Ἀσκληπιοῦ δύο παῖδε
ἰητῆρ' ἀγαθώ, Ποδαλείριος ἠδὲ Μαχάων.   B 731.

[2]   Μαχάονα δεῦρο κάλεσσον
φῶτ' Ἀσκληπιοῦ υἱὸν ἀμύμονος ἰητῆρος.   Δ 193.

[3]   πὰρ δὲ Μαχάων
βαῖν', Ἀσκληπιοῦ υἱὸς ἀμύμονος ἰητῆρος.   Λ 517.

[4] Δ 219.

edge of herbs and the art of healing, lived at a later time in eastern Thessaly.[1] The art of the Asklepiadæ differs not at all in kind from that of the pupils of Chiron. There is no hint of the intervention of a healing god, but purely natural methods are in use. The dream-oracle, which is the universal characteristic of the Asklepios cult, is entirely wanting. Machaon and Podaleirios are merely surgeons. In the warlike age which Homer presents, the knowledge of cleansing, binding and healing wounds was of the utmost importance. All the warriors were skilled in surgery, but the Asklepiadæ were the most famous. Clearer evidence that Asklepios was at this time located in Thessaly was established by O. Müller.[2] This line of argument depends upon the actual cult, usually a safer basis of reasoning than tradition, which is, generally speaking, the product of ritual. According to Müller the tribe of Phlegyans, which had come from the north into Thessaly and Boeotia, introduced Asklepios, for wherever traces of this tribe are found, there is likely to be a shrine of Asklepios. Probably the name Paiŏnìa, anciently given to a section of Macedonia, afterwards known as Emathia, belongs under this head. The Latin usage of shortening the *o* of the adjective *Paeonius*, in verse, affords an analogy for the quantity of the antepenult, which is most likely due to the same cause. In the cult in Thessaly, however, there is no mention of Machaon and Podaleirios. The traditions which call Asklepios their father, come from the Peloponnesus and the islands of

---

[1] Karl Otfried Müller, Orchomenos u. d. Minyer, Breslau, 1844, p. 244. The name Chiron has been thought to refer to a life in a poor and mountainous country, διὰ τὸ ἐν χείροσι καὶ ὀρεινοτέροις τόποις διάγειν. Et. M. 810, 33. Liddell and Scott connect the word with χειρουργός, the meaning of which changes from its use in classical Greek as an *artificer* to mean a *physician* in the Roman period. But no form of the compound χειρ-εργ- appears in Homer, nor in fact before Thucydides. Fick, Die gr. Personennamen, p. 88, derives the word from χείρ, giving it the meaning of *workman*. Is it not correct to consider that the frequent allusions in literature to Chiron in connection with healing may have led to the change in signification of the word χειρουργός?

[2] Orchomenos, p. 194 ff.

the Aegean.   Here the two are connected with Asklepios in
worship, and often stand alone in the same relation to healing.
Manifestly their connection with Asklepios was not original.
The passages of the Iliad which call them his sons, are of later
origin than the body of the poems,[1] and of these only
one assigns them to a Thessalian home.   We cannot be wrong
in denying them a place in northern Greece.   True, rumors of
Asklepios may have come from Thessaly to the Ionian coast,
but only as hero, not as divinity.   The main story belonged in
some region where Machaon and Podaleirios were honored,
while the divine nature of Asklepios was not known in the
north until succeeding centuries brought his worship into
connection with the southern deities of similar character.
Wilamowitz has located the region from which came the
stories of the Asklepiadæ as Kos.   It may be of interest
briefly to review his arguments.

The place which claims Machaon as founder of the state,
and from very early times honored the Asklepiadæ, was this
small island.   There are few traditions which connect Asklepios
with it.   The mother of Machaon, son of Asklepios, was a
daughter of Merops, a king of Kos.[2]   But a corrupt fragment
of the Ἰλίου πόρθησις quoted by the Scholiast on Λ 515 appears
to make Poseidon the father of the two heroes,[3] and a paraphrase in the commentary of Eustathios shows he had reason
to believe in a genealogy other than the orthodox.   Welcker
rejects the reading of the first line, and considers it wholly

---

[1] Wilamowitz, Isyllos von Epidauros, p. 45 ff.

[2] Μαχάων δὲ οὗτος υἱὸς Ἀσκληπιοῦ καὶ Ἀρσινόης ἢ Κορωνίδος, κατὰ δέ τινας Ἠπιόνης
τῆς Μέροπος, κατὰ δὲ Ἡσίοδον Ξάνθης. Sch. Δ 195.

[3] τοῦτο ἔοικε καὶ Ἀρκτῖνος ἐν Ἰλίου πορθήσει νομίζειν ἐν οἷς φησίν ·

Αὐτὸς γάρ σφιν ἔδωκε πατὴρ [ἐννόσχαιος πεσεῖν]
ἀμφοτέροις, ἕτερον δ᾽ ἑτέρου κυδίον᾽ ἔθηκε ·
τῷ μὲν κουφοτέρας χεῖρας πόρεν ἔκ τε βέλεμνα
σαρκὸς ἐλεῖν τμῆξαί τε καὶ ἕλκεα πάντ᾽ ἀκέσασθαι,
τῷ δ᾽ ἄρ᾽ ἀκριβέα πάντ᾽ εἰνὶ στήθεσσιν ἔθηκεν
ἀσκοπά τε γνῶναι καὶ ἀναλθέα ἰήσασθαι
ὃς ῥα καὶ Αἴαντος πρῶτος μάθε χωομένοιο
ὄμματα τ᾽ ἀστράπτοντα βαρυνόμενόν τε νόημα.

wrong to connect the Asklepiadæ with any but Asklepios.[1]
But whichever reading is the correct one, the fact that
Eustathios had reason to consider that the Asklepiadæ were
of a different origin from the one usually accepted is interesting, suggesting as it does that the sons and not the father were
original in Kos, and that the legends of their parentage were of
comparatively late growth. To explain the presence of a hero,
the Greek gave him a god as a father either Poseidon, whom the
seafarers of Kos might naturally choose, or Asklepios, emphasizing the most famous characteristic of the traditional founders
of the state.

We have further stories of Machaon's connection with Kos,
while Podaleirios is in every case subordinate. The two
allusions to the latter in the Iliad are interpolations, and
the prominence of Machaon, both as warrior and physician,
goes to show that he is original and that the brother is a
later invention, although a commentator tries to account for
the prominence of Machaon on the ground of the greater
need of his skill in treatment of wounds.[2] Pausanias speaks
of the death of Machaon at the hands of Eurypylos, giving
as his authority the μικρὰ Ἰλιάς.[3] "That is why, as I myself
know, in the rites in the temple of Asklepios at Pergamon,
they begin with the Hymns of Telephos, but make no reference
in their singing to Eurypylos, nor will they name him at all
in the temple, because they know he was the murderer of
Machaon."[4] Although Eurypylos is here son of Telephos
and thus a native of Mysia, the Catalogue[5] calls Kos Εὐρυ-

---

[1] Welcker, Ep. Cyc. II. p. 525.

[2] Agamemnon calls Machaon alone. οὐ καλεῖ δὲ ἄμφω, ὅτι ὁ μὲν περὶ τὰ τραύ-
ματα, ὁ δὲ περὶ τὰ ἄλλα ἦν νοσήματα. Sch. Δ 193. Cf. Sch. Λ 515. Wilamowitz
suggests that Podaleirios may be the eponymous hero of the Karian town Ποδά-
λεια, who in some way came to be associated with Machaon in the neighboring
island, to serve as a double, as in many hero cults.

[3] Μαχάονα δὲ ὑπὸ Εὐρυπύλου τοῦ Τηλέφου τελευτῆσαί φησιν ὁ τὰ ἔπη ποιήσας τὴν
μικρὰν Ἰλιάδα. Paus. III. 26, 9. For Eurypylos see Strabo XIII. 1, 7.

[4] Paus. III. 26, 10.

[5] B 677.

πύλοιο πόλις, so that the conflict of Machaon and Eurypylos was historically for the mastery of the island, an event dramatically transferred to the Trojan siege.

A second struggle is indicated by the stories of the Dorian Herakles who subdues the king and marries his daughter. He there becomes the father of the eponymous hero of Thessaly,[1] who himself is the father of Antiphos and Pheidippos who lead the forces from Kos. The national heroes of Kos, the Asklepiadæ, represent Thessaly and return there after the fall of Troy. Like the death of Machaon at the hands of Eurypylos is that of Eurypylos by Neoptolemos, a son of Phthian Achilles, whose family was closely connected with Kos. Lesbos is intimately joined with Kos, and with Phthia as well. Triopas in Knidos has the same genealogy[2] which Asklepios has according to Eustathios.[3] This gives a Thessalian origin to both from Lapithas, son of Apollo and Stilbe. This Triopas came to Thessaly from the Chersonese to aid the sons of Deucalion in expelling the Pelasgians. Afterwards he incurred the enmity of the people by cutting down the sacred grove of Demeter to build a temple, and was forced to flee to Knidos to whose headland, Triopium, he gave his name.

Wide objects to finding the point of union of the traditions in Kos, on the ground that the Asklepios cult in Kos is not so old as assumed. Traditionally, the worship of the god was brought from Epidauros to Kos, thus being two removes from Thessaly. The coins and inscriptions which relate to the cult are late.[4] The objection seems well founded, and yet there is no necessity for supposing that Asklepios as a god was known

---

[1] Κῶν ταύτην ἐλὼν Ἡρακλῆς μίγνυται Χαλκιόπῃ τῇ Εὐρυπύλου, καὶ ποιεῖ Θεσσαλόν. (Ἡρακλῆς) κατασυρεὶς δὲ εἰς Κῶν τὴν Μεροπίδα ἐκωλύθη ἐπιβῆναι τῆς νήσου ὑπὸ Εὐρυπύλου τοῦ Ποσειδῶνος βασιλεύοντος αὐτῆς. βιασάμενος δὲ καὶ ὡς λῃστὴς ἐπιβὰς ἀνεῖλε τὸν Εὐρίπυλον καὶ τοὺς παῖδας αὐτοῦ, μιγεὶς δὲ τῇ θυγατρὶ αὐτοῦ Χαλκιόπῃ Θεσσαλὸν ἐγγέννησεν. Sch. Ξ 255.

[2] Diodor. V. 61.

[3] Eustath. ad B 729.

[4] S. Wide, Lakonische Kulte, p. 195, note 5.

in Kos in Homeric times, even if the early colonists from Thessaly brought tales of this hero, of which traces are found in the later traditions of the island. The evidence goes to show an early connection between Thessaly and Kôs, but not the establishment of the Asklepios cult by the Thessalians.[1]

---

[1] Paton and Hicks, The Inscriptions of Cos, p. 347.

CHAPTER II.

ASKLEPIOS AS AN EARTH SPIRIT.

THE ritual and myths of Asklepios include many contra-
dictory features, and a superficial consideration of the cult in
its developed form shows a confusion out of which it seems
difficult to select the original elements. In one locality
Asklepios is worshipped with τράπεζα and κλίνη, and in
another he is the god of light, Αἰγλαήρ and Ἀγλαόπης.
Here he is the personification of healing in a water-cure
establishment, there he is the patron god of a city. He
has characteristics of almost all the gods, and to place him
in any one of the categories of the deities of the Greek
world, would be to ignore features which belong elsewhere.
It is necessary to distinguish between the essential and
unessential elements in order to determine what is really
Asklepiean. For example, in the case of the attributes,
tablet and rolls are symbols of the human science of healing
and are manifestly later than the conception of Asklepios as
a deity who heals by miracle. The same is true of the globe
and sceptre, attributes which have no place with a deity until
he becomes a wide-ruling god. The serpent on the other
hand is invariably present, in all times and places and is
evidently an essential attribute. In the ritual, all those
features are unessential which relate to the god as a divinity
of a whole people, as such usages grew up after the union
of local cults. Such, for example, are the yearly festivals
with attendant games and processions, and the intricate
machinery of the priesthood. But the consultation of the
oracle by dreams is an essential feature and from it the
original nature of the god may be known.

The superstitions in regard to dreams are too ancient and
well-known to need any extended discussion. The popular

beliefs in the oracular nature of dreams is the result of the
conception of the twofold man — the body which is seen,
and the spirit which is unseen.   Death and sleep separate
these two.   After death the spirit does not return, but after
sleep the spirit remembers what has occurred in its absence.
Among the Indo-European peoples the spirit after death was
believed to go into the earth, where the bodies were laid to
rest, and the spirit lived in a dreamy sort of existence.   This
is the familiar Homeric conception of death.   "Even as so
he spake the end of death overshadowed him.   And his soul,
fleeting from his limbs, went down to the house of Hades,
wailing its own doom, leaving manhood and youth." [1]   There
is very little in Homer to show that there was a connection
between the departed and the survivors.   In the threat of
Sarpedon to become "a shame and a horror for all time" if
his body is dishonored by the Greeks,[2] and the appearance of
Patroklos to Achilles,[3] as well as the funeral rites of Patroklos,[4]
are traces of this belief.   The cult of the dead was well known
in succeeding centuries, and these references may record usages
which existed contemporaneously with Homer, with which,
however, he was not familiar.   The belief that the spirits of
the dead manifested themselves to the living in dreams was
closely connected with the belief in their underworld existence.
And that the dreams were the spirits themselves, is proved on
the one side by the fact that the earth, that is, the abode of
the dead, was the mother of dreams,[5] and on the other, that
dream oracles were referred only to those spirits which lived
in the earth, and the Chthonian gods, which is after all the
same thing.   The only divinities consulted in dreams were

---

[1] Ὣς ἄρα μιν εἰπόντα τέλος θανάτοιο κάλυψε·
ψυχὴ δ᾽ ἐκ ῥεθέων πταμένη Ἄϊδόσδε βεβήκει,
ὃν πότμον γοόωσα, λιποῦσ᾽ ἀδροτῆτα καὶ ἥβην.   Π 855–57.

[2] Π 498.   Cf. P 556, X 358 and λ 72 ff.

[3] Ψ 65 ff.   Compare the account of Gawain's ghost at the opening of
Tennyson's Passing of Arthur.

[4] Ψ.   [5] Eurip. Iph. Tau. 1262; Hec. 71.

Dionysos and Pluto, and these only in certain localities. In
Amphikleia in Phokis, the priest of Dionysos cured through
dreams,[1] and near Nysa was a cave of Pluto in which cures
were similarly performed.[2]   Parallel to the dream oracles of
these gods were similar oracles which tradition referred not
to a local manifestation of the general spirit, but to a spirit
which lived under the earth in a single place, and with whom
no communication was held in other localities.   The best
known of these cave-gods is Amphiaraos, whose oracle in
Oropos in Boeotia was frequented by notable persons in
classical times.   This seer foreknew his own death in the
siege of Thebes, but was compelled to take part, and was
swallowed into a chasm in the earth which was opened by
the thunderbolt of Zeus.   As the place of his disappearance
was Thebes, while the oracle was at Oropos, the scene of
the story was transferred to suit the cult.   The traditions
of the other oracles are similar, those of Trophonios, Kaineus
in Thessaly, Althaimenes in Rhodes, and Amphilochos in
Akarnania or Kilikia.[3]   The earth oracles were those which
were most commonly consulted about the future, and many
of the most celebrated oracles of the classical period were
originally of this character.   There can be no doubt that this
was the case at Delphi.   The consultation was by dreams at
night.   Pytho, the serpent, which always stands in close
relation to the earth-cult, defended the shrine against Apollo,
who triumphed and yet absorbed into his ritual a prominent
feature of the earth-oracle, so that the Delphic priestess
received her inspiration from the vapors which rose from a
cleft in the rock.[4]   Thraemer suggests that as the earth is

---

[1] Paus. X. 33, 11.   [2] Strab. XIV. 1, 44.
[3] E. Rohde, Psyche, p. 108 ff.   Other dream-oracles of less importance are
known.   Stengel in Müller's HB. V. 3, p. 56.
[4] μαντεῖον χθόνιον, etc.   Eurip. Iph. Tau. 1249–80.
φασὶ γὰρ δὴ τὰ ἀρχαιότατα Γῆς εἶναι τὸ χρηστήριον.   Paus. X. 5, 5.
πρῶτον μὲν εὐχῇ τῇδε πρεσβεύω θεῶν τὴν πρωτόμαντιν Γαῖαν, Aeschyl. Eumen. 1.
Cf. Aelian. Var. Hist. III. 1.

worshipped only as the dwelling of spirits, the traces of the
cult of Dionysos in Delphi go to prove that it was a dream
oracle of this god which was replaced by Apollo.[1] In Aigai
was a cave in which an earth oracle existed until late,[2] and
the earth was worshipped at Dodona with Zeus.[3]

Such, too, was Asklepios, an earth spirit manifesting himself
in dreams. Hypnos and Oneiros are connected with him as a
god of sleep.[4] Hence the art-type of Asklepios as a benevolent
and venerable man, and his attributes, which are those of the
Chthonian gods. Amphiaraos and Trophonios were honored
in his temples, and Iaso is indifferently the daughter of
Amphiaraos or Asklepios. The various forms of earth and
death cults were not at home among the Ionian tribes, so that
Homer either ignored the little which came to his ears from
the interior of Greece and Thrace, or treated the reappearance
of the dead as special miracles. Thus Asklepios as deity finds
no mention in the Epic, and his cult was confined to one region
or tribe until features were developed which made him more
famous than the other divinities of like origin. It is in connection with Asklepios as a Chthonian spirit that the presence
of the serpent is to be explained, both actually in the temples,
and as an attribute.

The peculiarities of the serpent tribe are such as to arouse
the interest and lively curiosity of even a casual observer of
nature, and many are the strange beliefs resulting from the
early observations of serpents and their habits. Of all earth's
creatures, the serpent in many ways is the least like a human
being, and so is most inexplicable and mysterious. The dwell-

---

[1] Roscher, Lex. d. Myth. art. Dionysos, p. 1033.

[2] Paus. VII. 25, 13; Pliny, N. H. 28, 147.

[3] Ζεὺς ἦν, Ζεὺς ἐστι, Ζεὺς ἐσσεται, ὦ μεγάλε Ζεῦ.
    Γᾶ καρποὺς ἀνίει, διὸ κλῄζετε ματέρα Γαῖαν. Paus. X. 12, 10.

[4] So Hypnos in Epidauros, Bau. Aus Epid. p. 8; in Athens, CIA. II. 470;
while a statue of Somnus was dedicated to Asklepios in Reji, CIL. XII. 354.
Statues of Oneiros were dedicated in Lebena, Kaibel, 439; while there were statues
of both Hypnos and Oneiros in the Asklepieion at Sikyon, Paus. II. 10, 2; and
both are mentioned in Athens, CIA. III. 1, Add. et Corr. 132 a.

ing in the ground, the quick motion, the sudden appearance,
the staring, lidless eyes, the power of enduring hunger, its
longevity, the casting of its skin, and above all, its method
of killing and the peculiar attraction of its eyes, all these
found expression in superstition.   The worship of serpents
takes different forms in different countries.   In Scandinavia,
where it is an importation from the east, we know of the cult
as late as the sixteenth century.   "There are house serpents
which are accounted in the northern part of Sweden as house-
hold gods ; they are fed with sheep's and cow's milk, and to
hurt them is a deadly sin." [1]   The Zulus never destroy a
certain species of serpent believed to contain the spirit of
kinsmen,[2] and in many African tribes, human sacrifice, serpent
cult and ancestor-worship are found together.   The worship of
serpents was repressed in India by Buddhism, but the lower
classes still regard them as sacred.   If one is killed, a piece
of money is put into its mouth and its body burned to avert
evil.   Some Brahmans keep the skin of a Nâg in one of their
sacred books.

Independent of any connection with the Greek healing god,
in other parts of the world the serpent stands as a power
against sickness.   In Upper Egypt at Sheikh Haredi, a
serpent dwells in a cave and a virgin may go in and bring
him out twined about her neck to be carried to the bedside
of the sick, where he accomplishes wonderful cures.[3]   We
may recall the Hebraic account.   "Moses made a serpent
of brass and put it on a pole; and it came to pass, that if
a serpent had bitten any man, when he beheld the serpent
of brass, he lived." [4]   The serpent was later destroyed by
Hezekiah.   He "brake in pieces the brazen serpent that
Moses had made; for unto those days the children of Israel

[1] Olaus Magnus, XXI. 47.

[2] A. Lang, Myth, Ritual and Religion, I. p. 57.

[3] Norden, Travels in the East, II. p. 40; Wilkinson, Handbook of Egypt,
p. 301.

[4] Num. XXI. 9.

did burn incense to it." [1] The Nâga tribes of Cashmere, all of whose ancient temples are in honor of serpent-gods, have remarkable power in medicine, possessing nostrums, the knowledge of which has been handed down to them from antiquity.

The serpent was venerated because of its relation with the soul according to primitive thought. The relation was three-fold : first, the serpent was a fetish, the dwelling of the soul ; second, it was the soul ; and last, it was the symbol of the soul. This easily affords a clue to the connection of serpent and ancestor worship, for as a tribal ancestor dwells in the ground, so he comes out in the form of the animal which is preëminently the child of the ground.[2] So the Eddas conceive of the dead in the shape of serpents living among the roots of the trees, and Teutonic folk to this day offer food to the harmless house-snakes to gain their influence against fire and misfortune. The serpent is especially a protecting spirit and guardian of treasure. A serpent in which Erichthonios dwelt was sacred to Athena and protected the citadel, οἰκουρὸς ὄφις, and a monthly sacrifice of honey cakes was offered it. Before the battle of Salamis this offering was rejected, which was a sign to the Athenians that the goddess and the hero had abandoned the Acropolis.[3] The Romans had a similar belief. Aeneas sees in the serpent which appears at the grave of Anchises *geniumve loci famulumve parentis*. So the attendant Lares are thought of in serpent form.

As a manifestation of the dead, the serpent is the symbol of a hero, and of earth spirits in general, and hence is found with the Chthonian gods.[4] With Asklepios the serpent is usually only a ritualistic symbol and not in itself venerated. The god himself, however, was sometimes conceived under this form. A coin from Pergamon struck under Caracalla, bears on the

---

[1] 2 Kings, XVIII. 4.

[2] ὄφις, Γῆς παῖς. Hdt. I. 78.   [3] Hdt. VIII. 41.

[4] Mitth. d. Arch. Inst. II. 302, 307 ff., 315, 319 ff., 322, 375, 418, 444, 454, 459 A, 461 ff.; III. 100; V. 188 A, 387; IV. 156; VIII. 368.

reverse a figure of the Emperor in military dress with his right
hand raised to salute a serpent entwined around a tree, its head
towards the Emperor.   That the serpent who is here receiving
homage is Asklepios, is rendered certain both by the presence
of Telesphoros, and by comparison with another of Caracalla's
Pergamene coins, on which Telesphoros is represented upon a
pedestal placed as here between the Emperor and Asklepios,
who is depicted in the ordinary way.[1]   In the form of a serpent
Asklepios became the father of Aratos.[2]   No doubt many of
the patients believed that they saw the god in the sacred
serpents which were kept in the temples.

As the spirits of tribal ancestors were believed to dwell in
serpents, a number of legends arose about the foundation of
states by them.   Mantinea, for example, was so founded.
" But Antinoe, daughter of Kepheus, the son of Alous, inspired
by an oracle, led the men to this place, taking the serpent as a
guide." [3]   In this manner the worship of Asklepios was transferred from one place to another.   A serpent was carried, and
it was believed that in this form the god himself travelled.   So
a serpent was carried by mules from Epidauros to Sikyon.[4]
Another, which citizens of Epidauros Limera were carrying
from Epidauros, escaped from the boat to the shore.   Where

---

[1] W. Wroth, Asklepios and the Coins of Pergamon, p. 47.

[2] Paus. II. 10, 3; IV. 14, 7.

[3] Paus. VIII. 8, 4.   Other heroes appear in serpent shape : Kychreus in the
battle of Salamis, Paus. I. 36, 1 ; Sosipolis overcame the Arkadians in serpent
form for the Eleans, Paus. VI. 20, 5; so Erichthonios, Paus. I. 24, 7.   Heroes
are often represented as half-human and half-serpent, to symbolize their character
as αὐτόχθονες.   Such is especially the form of Erechtheus, for the Athenians were
particularly proud of their direct descent from Gaia.   The story of the Spartan
king Kleomenes is an illustration of the popular belief in the connection of the
dead and serpents.   After his body was crucified, a serpent was found coiled about
it, keeping off birds from it.   The Alexandrians supposed this to be a token that
Kleomenes had become a hero, until some wise man explained the phenomenon
by saying that as the bodies of oxen produce bees, and horses wasps, so a human
body produces serpents.   The author himself accepts this as fact, and ascribes the
popular idea to it.   Plut. Kl. 39.   Aelian gives another instance of a serpent
guarding the dead.   'Αποσπ. 82.

[4] Paus. II. 10, 3.

it landed, altars were built to Asklepios.[1]   The introduction
of the cult into Italy is similar.   In the year 291 B.C. a
pestilence fell upon the city of Rome, and, consulting the
Sibylline books, it was decided to bring Asklepios, but nothing was done that year except to decree a day of prayer to
him.[2]   Then the Delphic oracle declared that the god must
be carried to Rome.   In the shape of an enormous serpent
he was brought to the island in the Tiber, where his cult
was established.[3]

As an attribute, the serpent is especially frequent on coins.
Sometimes it is coiled about the staff, and often on the ground.
In a coin from Trikka the god is seated, feeding a serpent with
an object which may be a small bird.   Hygieia holding a *patera*
out of which the serpent seems about to eat is a familiar figure.
Mr. Wroth interprets this as a representation of serpent-divination, τῶν δρακόντων ἡ μαντική, in which she takes "an omen
as to the future health of her suppliants from the manner in
which the serpent receives the nourishment offered him."[4]
The serpent was believed from very remote times to be able
to foretell the future.   Melampos, the ancestor of Amphiaraos,
owed his gift of prophecy to young serpents which he cared
for after killing their parents.   Once, while he slept, they
licked his ears, from which time he understood the voices
of birds, and could prophesy.[5]   There is a similar legend in
regard to Kassandra and Helenos.   It is then possible that
the serpent was used in the way hinted above, but it was
not at all unusual that a god should be represented feeding
a sacred animal, and there is no literary evidence for the

---

[1] Paus. III. 23, 7.   [2] Livy, X. 47, 7; XXIX. 11, 1.
[3] Ovid, Met. XV. 622 ff.
[4] W. Wroth, Hygieia, Jour. Hell. Stud. 1884, p. 92 ff.   There is sometimes a
pine-cone on the patera, or Hygieia holds a cone in her hand.   The cone is frequently found in connection with the god on account of its healing properties.   A
statue at Sikyon represented the youthful Asklepios holding a pine-cone in the
hand; and a relief from Athens has the serpent staff, with two large fruits on one
side, and two cones on the other.
[5] Apollod. I. 9, 11.

practice of serpent-divination in this cult.   Serpents were
kept, however, in many and perhaps all of the sanctuaries.
In Alexandria they were carefully tended in the temple. [1]
In Epidauros the serpents were called παρεῖαι, or " puffy-
cheeked."   Aelian describes them as reddish-brown, fiery in
color, sharp-sighted, with a broad mouth.   The bite is not
dangerous ; the snakes are tame and sacred to Asklepios.[2]
Pausanias says they were thirty cubits long.[3]   In Titane
serpents were kept at the entrance of the sanctuary so that
it was necessary before entering to feed them to divert their
attention.[4]   Similarly, cakes were thrown to the serpents
before going into the cave of Trophonios.[5]   In Kos the
suppliants left cakes for the serpents after the omens were
declared.[6]   The use of serpents in healing is elsewhere
discussed.

At the time when the belief existed that sickness was an
evil demon, or the work of one, there was also the companion
idea that a good spirit could avail against the bad.   Hence it
came about that the aid of earth spirits was sought particularly
in cases of illness.   A secondary reason was that most of the
known remedies came from the ground.   It thus happened that
the peculiar province of departed heroes was to heal the sick,
and when a hero had no special cult or importance, it was most
natural that he received honor in a sanctuary of some healing divinity of greater importance.   Hence we find the temple
of Asklepios filled with statues of heroes, or some hero is
worshipped with him.   In many cases the Asklepios cult
replaced an older hero cult and made room for the hero in
the new shrine.[7]   The hero cult assumed greater proportions
in this respect than that of the greater Chthonian gods,[8] and

---

[1] Aelian, H. A. XVI. 39.
[2] Aelian, H. A. VIII. 12.   Cf. Demosth. 313, 25.
[3] Paus. II. 28, 1.   [4] Paus. II. 11, 8.
[5] Arist. Clouds, 507.   [6] Herond. IV. 91.
[7] Milchhöfer, Reliefs von Votivträgern in Jahrb. d. kais. deut. Arch. Inst. II. 23 ff.
[8] Roscher, Lex. d. Myth. art. Heros. p. 2481 ff.

in some way the oracle of Asklepios was more renowned than any of the others, and subordinated all functions to its importance as healing oracle. Traces of the general oracle, however, are found in late times. In Athens and Sikyon Asklepios was not consulted exclusively in cases of disease. Aristides gives evidence on this side, while from Epidauros come the stories of the lost child and the broken jar.

Beyond the rite of sleeping in the temple, there is little in the general procedure which refers to the Chthonian nature of Asklepios. Certain sacrifices were such as the lower-world gods received. The preliminary cake sacrifice which was offered in Athens, Titane and Kos has a Chthonian meaning, and the entire consumption of the flesh offerings has a similar significance.[1] The sacrifice of the cock is often mentioned, and has special significance, as it is a characteristic offering to underground spirits.

So far, I have spoken of the Chthonian nature of Asklepios without attempting to determine its limitations. It has been shown he was an earth spirit, and as such he was the soul of an ancestor whose descendants did him honor. Such, in a special form, was the hero cult of which there is mention from the latter half of the seventh century. I can see no reason why the Chthonian gods should not have had the same origin, the difference between hero and Chthonian god depending on the antiquity of the cults. On this basis Asklepios may be one or the other as one thinks of the age of the cult. One mark binds him with the gods rather than heroes. Asklepios was connected with a tribe rather than a locality. Müller identified Asklepios with Trophonios, who was a god of the Phlegyans in the same sense. In Lebadeia Trophonios appears with the attributes of Asklepios,[2] and Cicero gives them a common ancestry.[3]

---

[1] See Chap. VII. p. 80, and Stengel in Müller's HB. V. 3, pp. 69, 73.

[2] Paus. IX. 39, 3.

[3] Cic. de Nat. Deor. III. 22.

In the growth of the myths about Asklepios there were two things to account for: first, the tribal name; and second, the god. That the name of the god did not correspond to that of the tribe shows that he was somewhat higher than the eponymous tribal gods, as Herakles, Epidauros or Thessalos. Phlegyas was the name given to the founder of the race, just as Lapithas stood at the head of the Lapithae. Asklepios stands in the same relation to both tribes, and the two may have been identical, especially if we acknowledge the derivation of the one name from φλεγυᾶν, and of the other from λαπίζειν — the *boasters*. The least complicated of the Asklepios legends connects him with Trikka, a village in the western part of Thessaly, on the slope of a hill by the river Lethaios, a tributary of the Peneios. In the Catalogue of Ships, the sons of Asklepios come from Trikka and rocky Ithome, a town which lies south-east of Trikka.[1] The commentary of Eustathius is as follows: they say that the Asklepiadae are of the race of Lapithas, for Lapithas was the son of Stilbe and Apollo, and his grandson (Asklepios) was the son of Apollo and the nymph Koronis. Strabo says in Trikka there was a very ancient and famous sanctuary of Asklepios,[2] and mentions it as the birthplace of Asklepios. "There is another river of this name (Lethaios) in Gortyn and by Trikka, where Asklepios is said to have been born."[3] Little else is known of the cult in this part of Thessaly. The god bore the name Τρικκαῖος in Gerenia,[4] and the shrine is mentioned in the Epidaurian pæan. The coins from Trikka on which the god is represented, date from the fourth century.

Now had the Phlegyans and Lapithae fashioned their own mythology, Phlegyas or Lapithas would have been the son

---

[1] B 729 ff. Cf. Δ 201–2.

[2] ἔστι δ' ἡ μὲν Τρίκκη, ὅπου τὸ ἱερὸν τοῦ Ἀσκληπιοῦ τὸ ἀρχαιότατον καὶ ἐπιφανέστατον. Strab. IX. 5, 17.

[3] ἕτερος δ᾽ ἐστὶ Ληθαῖος ὁ ἐν Γορτύνῃ καὶ ὁ περὶ Τρίκκην, ἐφ᾽ ᾧ ὁ Ἀσκληπιὸς γεννηθῆναι λέγεται. Strab. XIV. 1, 39.

[4] Strab. VIII. 4, 4.

of Asklepios, for each tribe was proud of divine descent. But as this is not the case, and Asklepios is made the son of the tribe, the conclusion is that the myth sprang up outside of the family.[1] However the Phlegyans may have regarded their chief divinity, the first known attempt at giving him a genealogy made him only a man. The original myth was probably that which is least often cited, and only in late times. Cicero tells of an Aesculapius who was the son of Koronis and Valens, which is the Latin fashion of interpreting the name Ischys occurring in the Asklepios-Apollo legends. The Ischys story is closely interwoven with the Apolline myths, and as it will be seen that the Apollo connection was late, the earliest form of the story was that Asklepios was the son of Koronis and Ischys, in Thessaly.[2] The conflict between the Phlegyans and the followers of Apollo for the possession of Phokis resulted in a blending of the tribes and of the cults. Asklepios here became the son of the younger god. There are two reasons for the ready adoption of Asklepios by Apollo. Though the nature of the gods was different, and the ritual also, yet the importance of the oracle in both cases, and the relation of each to healing furnished two points of correspondence. The consequence was that many Apollo features were incorporated into the Asklepios cult. Such, for example, is the epithet Παιάν, and possibly ἀγλαός, though this is more likely to have come from the Helios cult. Ἄναξ, δεσπότης, ἄριστος, ἰήιος, ἤπιος (ἠπιόχειρ, ἠπιόφρων), κοίρανος, μάκαρ and χάρμα βροτοῖς come probably from Apollo.[3] Asklepios and Apollo were worshipped side by side in many towns, and statues

---

[1] O. Müller, Prolegomena, p. 271.

[2] Wide takes the view that the origin was Arkadian. Lakon. Kult., p. 197.

[3] That the epithet αἰγλήτης, which Apollo has on the island Anaphe, is taken from Asklepios, as Wilamowitz supposes, seems somewhat clumsy, especially if these "light" elements in the Asklepios cult are themselves taken from the Helios cult. Why should not Apollo adopt the epithets of Helios at first hand just as Asklepios did? See Wide, Lakon. Kult., p. 192, note 3.

of one were frequently placed in the temples of the other. Apollo takes the second name Maleatas, from a god brought with Asklepios from the north, and under this name shares the honors in Epidauros.[1]

The myths which sprang up after the welding of the two cults tended more and more to subordinate the older Thessalian god. A set of traditions which is connected with the eastern part of Thessaly is found in a few fragments of Hesiod, the Homeric Hymn to Asklepios, and the elaborated version of Pindar in the third Pythian Ode.

Koronis, the mother of Asklepios, is one of the five Hyades,[2] named by other authors as well as by Hesiod. Strabo says that the home of the Aenians was in the Dotian plain, near the lake which was once called Perrhaibia and Ossa, but now Boibeis, in the middle of Thessaly, surrounded by hills, and that Hesiod tells of a "maiden who lived on these twin holy hills in the plain opposite the Amyros abounding in grapes, and dipped her feet in the waters of the Boibeis."[3] Leake identifies this hill with a double ridge rising suddenly from the middle of the plain, between whose peaks lies a village which has been called both Dotion and Lakereia.[4] Phere-

---

[1] Isyl. v. Epid. p. 98 ff. Ap. Mal. is worshipped in Sparta, Paus. III. 12, 8, and on Mt. Kynortion in Epidauros, Paus. II. 27, 7. Ap. Maloris is found in Lesbos, Thuc. III. 3. Two small bronzes, one of a warrior and one of a goat, have been found in Kynuria, each bearing an inscription to Maleatas. Mitth. d. Arch. Inst. III. p. 17, and pl. 1; BCH. 1878, p. 355; IGA. 57, 89. An inscription from Peiraeus records an offering to Apollo and Maleatas. CIA. II. 3, 1651. See Preller-Robert, Gr. Myth. I. p. 252, note 4; Blass in Jahrb. für Phil. 1885, p. 822 ff.

[2]   Νύμφαι χαρίτεσσιν ὁμοῖαι,
Φαισύλη ἠδὲ Κορωνὶς εὐστέφανὸς τε κλέεια
Φαιώ θ' ἱμερόεσσα καὶ Εὐδώρη τανύπεπλος,
ἃς 'Τάδας καλέουσιν ἐπὶ χθονὶ φῦλ' ἀνθρώπων.   Hes. Frag. CLXXXI.

[3] Ἡ οἴη Διδύμους ἱεροὺς ναίουσα κολωνοὺς
Δωτίῳ ἐν πεδίῳ πολυβότρυος ἀντ' 'Αμύροιο
νίψατο Βοιβιάδος λίμνης πόδα παρθένος ἀδμής.
          Hes. Frag. CXLI. in Strab. IX. 5, 22 and XIV. 1, 40.

[4] Leake, Northern Greece, IV. p. 420.

kydes said that Koronis lived in Lakereia at (πρός) the sources of the Amyros,[1] a statement which shows his knowledge of geography to be at fault, for the Amyros flows westward and empties into Boibeis opposite the Dotian plain, as Hesiod correctly said.

The second bit of Hesiod relating to Koronis is the crow fable. "To Apollo indeed came the crow, and told her unseen act to Phoibos of the unshorn hair, when Ischys, son of Elatos, married Koronis, daughter of the god-born Phlegyas."[2] The tradition of the death of Asklepios is also found in Hesiod :

> "The mighty father both of gods and men
> Was filled with wrath, and from Olympus top
> With flaming thunderbolt cast down and slew
> Latona's well-loved son — such was his ire."[3]

All that remains then of the version of Hesiod is the home of the maiden, and her marriage with Ischys, son of Elatos, the knowledge of which is carried by the crow to Apollo, and the death of Asklepios. The death of Koronis and Ischys was in Hesiod's account, for Pherekydes in quoting the story gives the additional feature that Artemis killed

---

[1] Ὅτι δὲ ἡ Κορωνὶς ἐν Λακερείᾳ ᾤκει πρὸς ταῖς πηγαῖς τοῦ Ἀμύρου, Φερεκύδης ἐν πρώτῃ ἱστορεῖ. Pherekyd. Frag. 8, ed. Müller, in Sch. Pind. Pyth. III. 60.

[2] τῷ μὲν ἄρ' ἦλθε κόραξ, φράσσεν δ' ἄρα ἔργ' ἀίδηλα
Φοίβῳ ἀκερσεκόμῃ, ὅτ' ἄρ' Ἴσχυς ἔγημε Κορωνὶν
Ἐιλατίδης, Φλεγύαο διογνήτοιο θύγατρα.
. . . .
τῶν μὲν ἄρ' ἄγγελος ἦλθε κόραξ ἱερῆς ἀπὸ δαιτὸς
Πυθὼ ἐς ἠγαθέην, καί ῥ' ἔφρασεν ἔργ' ἀίδηλα
Φοίβῳ ἀκερσεκόμῃ ὅτι Ἴσχυς γῆμε Κορωνὶν
Ἐιλατίδης, Φλεγύαο διογνήτοιο θύγατρα.
                    Hes. Frag. CXLII. in Sch. Pind. Pyth. III. 14 and 48.

[3]   πατὴρ ἀνδρῶν τε θεῶν τε
χώσατ', ἀπ' Οὐλύμπου δὲ βαλὼν ψολόεντι κεραυνῷ
ἔκτανε Λητοΐδην, φίλον σὺν θυμὸν ὀρίνων.
Hes. Frag. CI. in Athenag. πρεσβ. ch. 29.   Cf. Philodem. De Rel. p. 17.   Λητοΐδην refers to Asklepios, not Apollo, for in Pind. Pyth. III. 67, the same name is used where there can be no doubt of its meaning.   Isyl. v. Epid. p. 64, note.

Koronis and many women with her, while her brother slew Ischys and took Asklepios to Chiron.

In the Hymn to Asklepios there is no addition:

> " With Aesculapius, the physician
> That cured all sickness, and was Phœbus' son,
> My nurse makes entry; to whose life gave yield
> Divine Coronis in the Dotian field
> (King Phlegyas' daughter) who much joy on men
> Conferred, in dear ease of their irksome pain.
> For which, my salutation worthy, King,
> And vows to thee paid, ever when I sing."

Pindar expands this outline in the third Pythian Ode:

" Of him was the daughter of Phlegyas of goodly steeds not yet delivered by Eileithyia, aid of mothers, ere by the golden bow she was slain at the hands of Artemis, and from her child-bed chamber went down into the house of Hades by contriving of Apollo. Not idle is the wrath of the sons of Zeus.

" She in the folly of her heart had set Apollo at naught, and taken another spouse without knowledge of her sire, albeit ere then she had lain with Phœbus of the unshorn hair, and bare within her the seed of a very god. Neither awaited she the marriage tables, nor the sound of the merry voices in hymeneal song, such as the bride's girl-mates are wont to sing at eventide with merry minstrelsy. But lo! she had longing for things otherwhere, even as many before and after. For a tribe there is most foolish among men, of such as scorn the things of home and gaze on things that are far off, and chase a cheating prey with hopes that shall never be fulfilled.

" Of such sort was the frenzied strong desire fair-robed Koronis harboured in her heart, for she lay in the couch of a stranger that was come from Arcady.

" But one that watched beheld her. For albeit he was at sheep-gathering Pytho, yet was the temple's king, Loxias, aware thereof, beside his unerring partner, for he gave heed to his own wisdom, his mind that knoweth all things; in lies it hath no part, neither in act nor thought may god or man deceive him.

" Therefore when he was aware of how she lay with the stranger Ischys, son of Elatos, and of her guile unrighteous, he sent his sister fierce with terrible wrath to go to Lakereia, for by the steep shores of the Boibian lake was the home of her virginity, and thus a doom adverse blasted her life and smote her down ; and of her neighbors many fared ill therefore and perished with her.   So doth a fire that from one spark has leapt upon a mountain lay waste wide space of wood.

" But when her kinsfolk had laid the damsel upon the pile of wood and fierce brightness of Hephaistos ran round it, then said Apollo : ' Not any longer may I endure in my soul to slay mine own seed by the most cruel death in company with its mother's grievous fate.'

" He said, and at the first stride he was there, and from the corpse caught up the child, and the blaze of the burning fiery pile was cloven before him asunder in the midst.

" Then to the Kentaur of Magnes he bare the child, that he should teach him to be a healer of the many plaguing maladies of man.   And thus all that came unto him, whether plagued with self-grown sores or with limbs wounded by the lustrous bronze or stone far hurled, or marred by summer heat or winter cold, these he delivered, loosing each from his several infirmity, or else he hung their limbs with charms, or by surgery he raised them up to health.

" Yet hath even wisdom been led captive of desire of gain.   Even him did gold in his hands glittering beguile for a great reward to bring back from death a man already prisoner thereto : wherefore the hands of Kronos smote the twain of them through the midst and bereft their breasts of breath, and the bright lightning dealt their doom." [1]

Three points of difference are at once noticeable between the accounts of Hesiod and Pindar.   First, the raven episode is ignored by the latter, and omniscient Apollo sees Koronis.[2] Second, there is a different interpretation of the relations of Koronis and Ischys.   Hesiod speaks of their marriage, while Pindar takes occasion to show the relation to be secret and guilty.   Additional blame is attached to Koronis in that Ischys is a stranger from Arkadia, while Hesiod only knows him as the son of Elatos.   The son of Elatos, however, may not necessarily be a son of the Arkadian.   It is true that a connection between Koroneia and Elateia in Arkadia might suggest such a union, but the Thessalian Elateia is more likely to have done so, especially as Elatos, one of the Lapi-

---

[1] Translation of E. Myers.
[2] Artemon in Sch. Pind. Pyth. III. 48.

thae, was the father of Kaineus[1] who was brother of Ischys.[2]
One of the fragments of Sophocles mentions the Thessalian
Elatos from Larissa.[3]   Third, the bribery of Asklepios is
given only by Pindar and the writers who depend upon him.
This was a sweet morsel for the church fathers, who rejoiced
to find a weak spot in the characters of the heathen divinities.
Hesiod honors Apollo above Asklepios, but while he elevates
Apollo, he does not degrade Asklepios.   To neither poet was
Asklepios a god, but to the older he was a hero, while in the
eyes of the younger, the life and fame of Asklepios existed
merely by the condescension of Apollo.

The story in Apollodorus is a paraphrase of the Hesiodic
account, for nothing is said of the Arkadian descent, and the
crow episode is given in full.[4]   The account of the marriage
in the absence of Apollo has been omitted, but the death of
Asklepios is given, as well as the anger of Apollo who is
compelled to serve Admetos as punishment for having killed
the Cyclops, forgers of the thunderbolts.   The latter part of
the story is at the beginning of the Alkestis of Euripides.
According to Pherekydes, Apollo does not kill the Cyclops,
but their sons.[5]   The connection of the Apollo-Admetos
story is so close that it was probably in Hesiod.

There are slight variations in the different accounts.   Apollodorus leaves us to believe that Koronis dies by the hand of
Apollo, which is contrary to the Greek belief about the death
of women.[6]   In the version of Ovid, Apollo kills Koronis,[7]
and Hyginus says that Ischys is killed by the bolt of Zeus.[8]

---

[1] Hygin. Fab. 14.

[2] Apollod. III. 10, 3.   Elatos was also the father of Dotia, after whom Dotion
took its name, Steph. Byz. art. Δώτιον; or of Dotis, who was the mother of
Phlegyas by Ares, Apollod. III. 5, 5.

[3] Soph. Frag. 348, ed. Nauck.

[4] Apollod. III. 10, 3, 6.

[5] Pherekyd. Frag. LXXVI. in Sch. Eurip. Alk. 1.

[6] Wilamowitz would amend the reading in Apollodorus so that it agrees with
Pherekydes.

[7] Ovid, Met. II. 605.   [8] Hygin. Fab. 202.

Hermes and not Apollo rescued the child from the flames in the legend as told by Pausanias.[1]

Many accounts exist of the dead who were raised by Asklepios, and two specify the means used. According to one, he derived power from the Gorgon's blood given him by Athena. What came from the left side he used for destroying, but that from the right side for the health and resurrection of men. In another tradition, it was said that he was shut up in a secret apartment in the house of Glaukos, pondering how to raise the master whom Zeus had struck with his bolt. A serpent glided into the room, and Asklepios raised his staff and killed it, whereupon a second serpent came in, and by laying an herb in the mouth of the first, brought it back to life. By the use of this herb Asklepios then recalled Glaukos.[2] Several other men are said to have been raised also.[3]

According to some traditions the cause of the death of Asklepios was healing, and not raising from the dead. Apollodorus says that Zeus feared the presumption of the healer, while according to Diodorus, Zeus slew him on account of a complaint from Hades that his realm was becoming depopulated.[4] There is a late legend that at the request of Apollo, Asklepios was placed among the stars where he is seen with the attribute of the serpent. Zeus also placed in the heavens the arrow with which the Cyclops were killed.[5]

Most of the features of the story are easily explained. The name Koronis was perhaps derived from Koronos and Koroneia in Thessaly, and with a play on the name suggesting the chattering crow, κορώνη λακέρυζα, she was localized in *Chatterton*, Λακέρεια. The possible connection of Elatos with this town, suggested by the tradition of the name of the plain, and his

---

[1] Paus. II. 26, 6.
[2] Apollod. III. 10, 3, 9; Tatian, Ad. Gr. XII.
[3] See General Index.   [4] Diodor. IV. 71.
[5] Hygin. Astr. II. 14 and 15.

daughter, localizes again the Ischys legend. The birth of
Asklepios is like that of Dionysos, and Hermes rescued many
of the children of the gods.[1] Chiron is the traditional
teacher of Thessalian heroes, and therefore of Asklepios.
Asklepios can fittingly die but in one way, by the bolt of
Zeus. But the fact that he dies at all, shows that he has
lost his divinity, although the manner of death is a distinction.[2] The traditions of the death would most conclusively
prove that he was never a god, were it not that evidence is
wanting to show that the cult and oracle were confined to
the place of his death. Pherekydes says that the death
occurred ἐν Πυθῶνι. If this were a cult tradition, the original
place of worship would have been here. But of an Asklepieion at Delphi there is no trace, and so important a cult
could scarcely pass unnoticed in Delphi of all places, so
rich in legend. Very naturally, the name Delphi was added
to the story, all of which was invented for the honor of Apollo.
There are other places where Asklepios was said to be buried.
The first is connected with the Ischys-Koronis descent, and is
Kynosoura, a village of Lakedaimon according to Hesychius,
though perhaps of Arkadia. It is not only doubtful where
the locality was, but it has no evidence in its favor, ritualistic or literary, except in late writers.[3] The genealogy con-

---

[1] Hermes took the infant Dionysos to the nymphs at Nysa, Welcker, Götterl.
II. 444; the Dioskuri from Pephnos to Pellana, Paus. III. 26, 2; Aristaios to
the Hours, Pind. Pyth. IV. 5, 9; and takes charge of Herakles and Ion, Eurip.
Ion, 1598.

[2] Plutarch says that a bolt fell into the grave of Lycurgus, which happened to
no one afterwards but to Euripides. "It was strong evidence for the admirers of
Euripides when that occurred for him alone which had happened previously to
one most beloved of the gods, and holy." The body of one killed by lightning
must be buried at the place of death, Artemid. Oneir. II. 9. Minucius Felix calls
the death of Asklepios his glorification. "Aesculapius, ut in deum surgat, fulmi-
natur." 22, 7. See Artemid. Oneir. II. 9. οὐδεὶς γὰρ κεραυνωθεὶς ἀτιμός ἐστιν
ὅπου γε καὶ ὡς θεὸς τιμᾶται. There was a tragedy called Asklepios, by Aristarchus
of Tegea. Suid. art. Ἀριστ.

[3] Clem. Alex. protr. II. 30; Io. Laur. Lyd. de Mens. IV. 90; Cic. de Nat.
Deor. III. 22, 57.

nected with it, however, can be trusted, for the combination
of the legends in which Apollo and Ischys are rivals speaks
for the crowding out of Ischys by the god. The second
burial place is in Arkadia, which is again connected with
a different genealogy, that of Arsippos-Arsinoe.[1] This is
again found in late writers and has only the name Arsinoe
to connect it with any of the Asklepios stories. Thraemer
suggests that some local hero was confused with the god.
The statement that Asklepios had a tomb in Epidauros is
of no especial value, for its author joins Hermes, Mars,
Venus, Herakles and Asklepios, claiming that the idolatrous
Greeks worshipped these mortals at the place of decease,[2]
which is so inaccurate that we should accept it with reserva-
tion, and follow the evidence from Epidauros itself. Strange
to say, with the exception of the localization of Pherekydes,
the graves were all in Peloponnesos, while none of the death
legends belong to southern Greece. I am therefore inclined
to attach little importance to so slight evidence for the hero-
cult, and find proof for it only in one Asklepieion, namely,
in Athens. The dream-god of the Thracian tribe gained a
new ancestry in Thessaly, and lost it again to become the
son of Apollo, and in legend a hero. The cult itself was
very little affected by the traditions of "heroism," although
in Athens it undoubtedly took this form. There are two
allusions to the Heroia which were celebrated every year in
Athens.[3] Plato called Asklepios the ancestor of the Athenians,[4] and Tertullian said that the Athenians paid divine
honors to Asklepios and his mother among their dead.[5]

---

[1] Io. Laur. Lyd. *loc. cit.*; Cic. *loc. cit.*

[2] Clement. Recog. X. 24.

[3] CIA. II. 1, Add. Nov. 453 *b* and *c*.

[4] ὁ ἡμέτερος πρόγονος 'Ασκληπιός · · ·. Plato, Sym. 186 E.

[5] Tertul. Ad. Nat. II. 14. In the theatre of Dionysos, the assignment of each
seat was inscribed upon it. One seat bears the words ἱερέως 'Ασκληπιοῦ, and a
third word, which is very obscure, and may be either ἥρωος or Παίωνος. Thræmer
in Roscher, Lex. d. Myth. p. 620; CIA. III. 263. Cf. 287.

Some reliefs from the Asklepieion so closely resemble steles
representing funeral banquets as to have led to the opinion
that they are really such, and that the sanctuary served as
well for burial as for healing.   The death-reliefs represent
the departed enjoying a banquet, either as in life, or, what
is more probable, in his further existence.   The dog lying
beneath the couch, and the horse standing by, may then well
recall an ancient custom of burying favorite animals with
their master.   Le Bas tried to explain the presence of the
horse in the similar reliefs of Asklepios as representing the
steed of Thanatos, which *would* have carried off the suppliant
had it not been for the interposition of the god!   This accords
with a popular belief of the Greeks of to-day, that Charon
rides about the country on horseback seizing the living and
transporting them to the other world.   It is not likely, however, that this is an original Greek, but a Slavonic conception.
The head of the horse is sometimes seen in a sunken square.
It is a forced explanation that it represents the animal looking
in at a window.   Heroes were honored by a death banquet
and we know that this was also the case in the Asklepios
cult in Athens, for one of the duties of the priest was to
arrange the table and spread the couches.[1]   On the couch
the statue was laid and a feast spread by its side, as is the
custom in hero-cults.   These reliefs then represent actual
scenes in the temple, and the artist used his discretion in
giving life to the statue of the god.   The reliefs so resembled
the funeral steles that conventional symbols were introduced.
The statue of Asklepios in Epidauros is similar to a relief
from a tomb in Patras.[2]   Similar banquet scenes are connected
with earth cult in Tarentum.[3]

Why the cult took this form in Athens and not in Epidauros
from which it was derived, or in the other offshoots of the

[1] CIA. II. 1, Add. Nov. 373 *b*; 453 *b* and *c*.
[2] Mitth. d. Arch. Inst. VIII. pl. 18.
[3] Arthur J. Evans, Tarentine Terracottas, in Jour. Hell. Stud. 1887, p. 1 ff.

original cult, is a problem whose solution must be sought not in the cult, but in the nature of the soil to which it was transplanted.

The introduction of a foreign divinity such as Asklepios among the Ionians implies an assimilation and compromise of cult. A Chthonian god must lose some of his importance when adopted by a people whose religious thought is wholly at variance with the ideas which underlie his worship. An earth cult is not natural to an Ionian tribe, and Asklepios was not important enough to displace the gods of the upper world. Through literature, Athens had long known the *hero* Asklepios. Every Athenian gentleman of the fifth century knew his Homer and Hesiod, and the city could not forget the Theban poet she had delighted to honor. The *man* was thus known before the *god*. Another reason for the accept· ance of Asklepios as hero rather than god lies in the fact that before his introduction the Athenians had been long familiar with a hero physician, and perhaps with more than one. Sophocles was at one time the priest of one of these, Alkon, who legend said had learned his art with Asklepios from Chiron.[1] Asklepios appeared to Sophocles and commanded him to write a pæan in his honor.[2] According to

---

[1] Anonym. Vit. Soph. 8, p. 128. Two inscriptions to ἥρως ἰατρός, CIA. II. 1, 403 and 404. See Hirschfeld in Hermes VIII, p. 350 ff., and Sybel in Hermes XX. p. 41 ff.

[2] Philost. Jun. Imag. 13, p. 17. This pæan continued long in use. Luc. Δημ. ἐγκώμ. 27. ᾽ οἱ δὲ ᾖδον ᾠδήν, ὁποῖος ὁ παιὰν ὁ τοῦ Σοφοκλέους, ὃν ᾽Αθήνησι τῷ ᾽Ασκλη-πιῷ ᾅδουσιν. Philost. Vit. Apoll. III. 17, p. 50. A stone found in the Asklepieion bears a fragment of a pæan which may be this one:

Σοφοκλέους.

[᾽Ω Φλεγύα] κούρα περιώνυμε, μᾶτερ ἀλεξιπό[νου · · ·]

[Φοῖβο]ς ἀκειρεκόμας · · · ἐναρίθμι[ον? · · ·]

· · · εσι[ν] εὐεπ[ίη].

CIA. III. 1, Add. et Corr. 171 g. Kumanudis and Bücheler both attribute this to Sophocles from its heading, while Dittenberger doubts that it is the work of the tragedian, for a comparison with 171 a shows that the name written above may be that of the dedicator. Sophocles was a common name in the Roman period. This is similar to 171 b, and no one would think that either an early composition, or the work of a great poet.

another story, Sophocles entertained Asklepios at his house [1] and built him an altar, for which he was given heroic honors after death under the name Δεξίων,[2] and his name brought great honor to the Asklepieion.[3]

The tendency of the Athenian cult was to localize Asklepios, while the very opposite course was followed in other parts of Greece. Here he was associated with heroes rather than with the higher gods,[4] while in Epidauros and elsewhere he is worshipped with Zeus, Apollo, Artemis, and so on. It is interesting to note that although in Athens the ritual was in part that of a hero, the pæans follow the version of Hesiod, but leave out the feature which justifies the usages. Asklepios is the son of Apollo and Koronis, but there is no hint of the Ischys legend, or of the death.

Another set of traditions is connected with Messenia. Here Asklepios was the child of Arsinoe, the daughter of Leukippos. The Messenians cherished this story and honored Arsinoe by calling a fountain in the Agora by her name. Pausanias considered this the least probable legend, and believed it to have been fabricated by Hesiod or some one else to please the Messenians, because Apollo in an oracular response acknowledged the child as his, borne by Koronis in Epidauros.[5] The claim rested on the evidence of the Catalogue, for there was an Ithome and an Oichalia in Messenia as well as in Thessaly, and near them a deserted place called Trikka. The Messenians were sure that Nestor would not have aided the wounded Machaon, had he not been a neighbor.[6] Sparta had a Hieron of Arsinoe on this account.[7] Apollodorus credited this story and placed it before the Thessalian. Asklepiades quoted from

---

[1] Σοφοκλεῖ δὲ καὶ ζῶντι τὸν Ἀσκληπιὸν ἐπιξενωθῆναι λόγος ἐστί. Plut. Numa, IV. ἢ τὸν Ἀσκληπιὸν Σοφοκλῆς ξενίζειν. Non Poss. 22. It is doubtful whether the altars alluded to in inscriptions were in the first or second temple. Mitth. d. Arch. Inst. II. 241. In the Vit. Soph. the altar was built in the τέμενος of Alkon.

[2] ἀπὸ τῆς τοῦ Ἀσκληπιοῦ δεξιώσεως. Et. Mag.

[3] τὸ ἀπὸ Σοφοκλέους ἐπιφανὲς Ἀσκληπιεῖον. Marin. Procl. 29.

[4] CIA. II. 1, 162, 470; III. 1, Add. et Corr. 132 a.

[5] Paus. II. 26, 7. [6] Paus. IV. 3, 2. [7] Paus. III. 12, 8.

Hesiod in support of it.[1]   His citation may be from the Catalogue of the Leukippidae which must have come from some
other hand than that of Hesiod; for the story contradicts the
Eoie, as here Arsinoe is mother not only of Asklepios, but
a daughter, Eriopis, and there was manifestly no second child
in the Thessalian version.   The general likeness shows a
dependence upon the Eoie.   Here is the rivalry of Apollo
and Ischys,[2] and the death of the Cyclops.   Aristides Milesius
tried to reconcile the Thessalian and Messenian versions by
considering Koronis another name of Arsinoe.[3]   Arsinoe,[4] as
well as Koronis,[5] is called the mother of Machaon.

Pausanias, in his description of Epidauros, collects the
various traditions of Asklepios, emphasizing particularly the
one current in Epidauros, a city sacred to him.   "They say
that Phlegyas came to the Peloponnesos on the pretext of
seeing the country, but really to spy out the population, and
see if the number of fighting men was large.   For Phlegyas
was the greatest warrior of that day.   But when he came to
the Peloponnesos his daughter followed him, who, though
her father knew it not, was with child by Apollo.   And when
she bare her child on Epidaurian soil, she exposed it on the
mountain called in our day Tittheion, but which was then
called Myrgion.   And as he was exposed there, one of the
she-goats feeding on the mountain gave him milk, and the
watch dog of the flock guarded him.   And Aresthanas, for
that was the name of the goat-herd, when he found the number
of goats not tallying and that the dog was also absent from
the flock, went in search everywhere, and when he saw the
child, desired to take him away, but when he drew near,
seeing lightning shining from the child, and thinking there
was something divine in all this, as indeed there was, he
turned away.   And it was forthwith noised abroad about the

---

[1] In Sch. Pind. Pyth. III. 14.   [2] Hom. Hymn. ad Ap. 208 ff.
[3] Arist. Mil. in Sch. Pind. Pyth. III. 14.   [4] Sch. Δ 195.
[5] Hygin. Fab. 97.

lad both by land and sea that he could heal sickness, and raise
the dead." This account differs materially from the Thessalian story. Here Phlegyas and his daughter are strangers,
though Epidauros claims to be the birthplace of the god.
There is no Ischys legend and nothing of the fate of Koronis.
On the other hand, the exposure of the child, the attendant
Aresthanas, the goat and dog, are not found in Thessaly.
This part of the story is duplicated in Thelpusa, where there
was a cult of Asklepios παῖς. Here a dove, τρυγών, brought
food to the child, a story easily connected with a monument
of Trygon which stood in the Hieron.[1] Evidently the child-
legend existed in the Peloponnesos before the northern traditions were adopted, and the goat and dog served to account
for certain features in the ritual which were not a part of
the northern cult. The goat was sacred, so the myth was
fashioned to account for it. The dog was sacred in Epidauros
as is known from the steles, and from the great statue of
Asklepios in Epidauros which is preserved only in tradition
and on coins. In this, the dog lies under the chair of the
god. The dog is found on a Thessalian coin of the second
century B.C., on which Asklepios is seated with a dog at his
feet.[2] Dogs were kept in Athens to guard the sacred treas-
ures,[3] and one is represented with Machaon, Podeleirios and
Asklepios on a relief from this city.[4] In the Cretan inscription, the zacore has charge of the κύνια τόα, which Baunack
interprets as κύνια ζόα, either figures of dogs which are appropriately left in the temple as offerings, or dogs themselves,[5]
which were kept in the Cretan Asklepieion, as in Athens,
Epidauros, and in Kypros.[6] It seems that the sacredness
of the dog was a local feature of the Epidaurian cult which
spread to the others. The date of the Thessalian coin shows

---

[1] Paus. VIII. 25, 11.   [2] Head, Hist. Num. p. 256.
[3] Aelian. H. A. VII. 13; Plut. De Sol. Animal. XIII. 11. Cf. CIA. II. 3, 1651.
[4] Le Bas, Voy. Arch. pl. 53, 2 ; Reinach in Rev. Arch. 1884, p. 129 ff.
[5] Philol. 1890, p. 596.
[6] Revue Critique, 1884, n. 37, p. 202; Aelian. H. A. VII. 13.

that the dog had no more original connection with the cult in this region than Hygieia and Telesphoros, occasional traces of whom are found in Thessaly. To account for the dog in Epidauros, the baby-god was given a watch-dog. We come nearer to the rest of the Peloponnesian legend in the pæan of Isyllos of Epidauros :

"Sing praises to Paian Apollo, ye people, dwellers in holy Epidauros, for thus the oracle was declared to the ears of our fathers, O Phoibos Apollo. They say that Zeus the father gave the muse Erato to Malos in sacred wedlock. And Phlegyas, a native of Epidauros, and living there, married the daughter whom Erato bore whose name was Kleophema. Then to Phlegyas was born a daughter, Aigle by name, who for her beauty was called Koronis. And Phoibos of the golden bow, the yellow-haired son of Leto, seeing her in the home of Malos, ended her maiden days in lovely marriage. Thee I praise. But in the fragrant enclosure Aigle bore a child to him, and the son of Zeus, and Lachesis, the noble mother, with the Fates, eased the pains of labor. Apollo called him Asklepios from his mother Aigle, the reliever of disease, giver of health, a great boon to mortals. Hail Paian, Paian Asklepios, increase thy native city, Epidauros, and send to our minds and bodies shining health. Hail, Paian, Paian."[1]

In disentangling the Thessalian and Epidaurian elements one can scarcely fail to be convinced by the reasoning of Wilamowitz. Koronis has nothing to do with Epidauros, but Aigle is Epidaurian, and a mother, Kleophema, is put in to fill up the circle. Originally, Aigle must have been the daughter of Malos who had dedicated an altar to Apollo Maleatas. The myths about the unfaithfulness of Koronis and the life and death of her son have here no place, and Aigle bears her child with the favor of the gods. Malos and Aigle were the only necessary factors in the Epidaurian tradition, the one to account for Maleatas, a "beiname" of Apollo, and the other for Asklepios. Erato was the necessary mother to account for Aigle and give her a lofty ancestry, as in Arkadia she is the wife of Arkas and mother of Elatos. Wide explains the relation of Aigle to Asklepios from the

---

[1] Baunack, Stud. I. 1, 84, 37 ff.

connection of the latter with Helios in Lakonia and Messenia.
Arsinoe, the daughter of Helios under the name Leukippos,[1]
is the mother or wife of Asklepios. In Gytheion, Asklepios
and Hygieia are joined in cult with Helios,[2] and also in
Epidauros.[3] Now Aigle figures as a Naiad and wife of Helios,
and the name Αἰγλάηρ by which Asklepios was called in
Lakonia not only corresponds in form to the name Aigle,
but in content to the epithets of Helios as φαέθων, ἠλέκτωρ
and πασιφαής. Asklepios coming from the north assumed
the epithet of Helios, whose cult was already in Lakonia,
and Aigle became his mother as in the cult pæan of Epidauros.
In this connection the many signs that Asklepios was a
"light" god and not an earth god, would be accounted for.
Lampetie, who belongs in the same category as Aigle, was
in one legend the wife of Asklepios,[4] Aglaïa was the mother
of Machaon by Asklepios,[5] and Aigle is the daughter in
Athens.[6] Here belong the epithets ἀγλαός,[7] ἀγλαότιμος,[8] the
name ἀγλαότης[9] and the "beinamen" αἰγλήτης and ἀσγελά-
τας which Apollo bears on Anaphe, which are to be referred
to the same origin. Whether the last two were borrowed
from Helios directly as Wide supposes, or indirectly according to Wilamowitz, is difficult to say. Undoubtedly, the
Asklepios cult assumed a "light" character as it traveled
southward.

The complex character of the cult in Southern Greece is to
be referred to the existence of healing gods or heroes before
the introduction of the Thessalian cult. Some of these healing divinities became the sons or grandsons of Asklepios,

---

[1] Maas, G. G. A. 1890, p. 346.   [2] CIG. 1392.
[3] Bau. 1 and 99.
[4] Hermipp. in Sch. Arist. Plut. 701.
[5] Quint. Smyrn. p. h. 6, 492.
[6] Hermipp. in Sch. Arist. Plut. 701; Aristid. 79, 5; Suidas, art. 'Ηπιόνη; CIA.
III. 1, Add. et Corr. 171 b; Pliny, N. H. 35, 137; Rev. Arch. 1889, p. 70.
[7] Mionnet, Description des Médailles antiques Grecques et Romaines, VI. 572, 70.
[8] Orph. Hymn. 67, 6.   [9] Hesych.

and in some cases Asklepios assumed as second name the name of a supplanted hero.

A Phoenician god was identified with Asklepios, and under his name connected with eastern divinities on the island of Delos.[1] The genealogy was borrowed and given to this new Asklepios, who bore some resemblance to the Greek god.[2] The existence of the Asklepiastai in Athens may show that the oriental god was known there too, for such societies were generally formed in honor of a foreign deity.

---

[1] BCH. VI. 498; VII. 366.
[2] Damasc. Βίοϲ Ἰϲ. in Phot. Bibl. II. 352; Philo Bybl. Fr. X.

CHAPTER III

THE SANCTUARIES OF ASKLEPIOS.

THE peculiar features of the Asklepieia had their origin in the fact that the temples served a double purpose. So far as they were places of worship, they differed little from the temples of other gods, for from the time when temples were erected to Asklepios he had lost to a large extent the characteristics of Chthonian gods, and only hints of the primitive status remained. His sanctuaries became health resorts, and as such were famous. Hence the most popular Asklepieion was that which was so contrived as to combine the advantages of a healthful location with the impressive administration of ritual.

The location of an Asklepieion was chosen where fresh air abounded, and the eye was charmed by the variety of the scenery. No other god chose so wholesome and pure a spot as did Asklepios at Pergamon.[1] In Carthage the Asklepieion stood on the Acropolis.[2] The most famous resorts were at a little distance from a town, as in Epidauros, Kos, Pergamon and Rome. The Athenian Asklepieion was crowded on the southern slope of the Acropolis, but there was a second one at Peiraeus.[3] Little is known of this seaside resort, and as proofs of its existence we have only two indirect allusions

---

[1] Aristid. 409, 9.   [2] Appian. VIII. 130; Strab. XVII. 3, 14.

[3] Sch. Arist. Plut. 621. The location of the Asklepieion at Peiraeus is like that at Lebena, which is a harbor town of Crete, about ten miles south of Gortyna. Sybel, Mitth. d. Arch. Inst. X. p. 97, attempts to prove that the outer Asklepieion was not at Peiraeus, but at Phalerum, basing his belief on Pliny, N. H. II. 225: *quae in Aesculapii fonte Athenis mersa sunt, in Phalerico redduntur.* Phalerus was the son of Alkon, a myth to establish a connection between the older harbor and the spring of the Asklepieion. Plutarch theorizes about the choice of the location of the Asklepieia. "Why is the sanctuary of Asklepios outside of

to it, and a single dedicatory inscription to Apollo Maleatas, Hermes, and the healing nymphs, which may have come from an Asklepieion or not, though evidently from a shrine of a healing divinity.[1]   The site of the city shrine at present is anything but health-giving, presenting itself to the full glare of the sun.   But in the earlier days a grove overhung the temple, while the steep hill behind kept off the chilling winds of the cold season.   The temple of Asklepios, as that of a Chthonian deity, should have stood on a level space, but the rule is only observed in Epidauros.   Usually the enclosure had but one entrance, πρόπυλον, on the west side, which was closed with doors, θυρώματα.   In Athens there were two entrances, corresponding to two temples within the same precinct.[2]   The exact site of the two is not proved.[3]   It seems that an old temple was never destroyed, but fell into neglect upon the erection of a second.[4]   This was also the case in the precinct of Dionysos in Athens, the two temples of the Kabeiri in Samothrace, and of Athena on the Acropolis.

Certain features existed in every Asklepieion which per-petuated in modified form the characteristics of the original place of worship.   As a reminiscence of the shaded mountain cave, the τέμενος, which was bounded by a wall, πρόβλημα, included a grove, and so gained another name, ἄλσος, which, in Epidauros at least, is used for the whole ground adjoining

---

the city?   Was it because they reckoned it a wholesome kind of living outside of the city?   For the Greeks have placed the edifices belonging to Asklepios for the most part on high places, where the air is pure and clear. . . .   For the temple of Asklepios is not close by that city (Epidauros), but at a great distance from it."   Quaest. Rom. 94.

[1] Ἀσκληπιὸς ὁ ἐν ἄστει.   CIA. II. 1, Add. Nov. 477 b.   First century B.C. Ἀσκληπιεῖον τὸ ἐν ἄστει.   CIA. II. 1, Add. Nov. 159 b.   Fourth century B.C. For ἄστυ, see E. Curtius, Mitth. d. Arch. Inst. II. p. 53 ff.   Cf. p. 176, note.   CIA. II. 3, 1651.

[2] CIA. II. 1, Add. et Corr. 489 b.

[3] For the relative positions of the Asklepieia, see Köhler, Mitth. d. Arch. Inst. II. p. 171 ff.; 231 ff.   Girard, L'Asclèpieion D'Athènes, pp. 4–15.

[4] Köhler, ibid. p. 174.

the temple.[1] Here the trees overhung the very temple.[2] In Kos was a grove,[3] in part of cypresses[4] as in Titane.[5] Olive trees grew about the altars in Epidauros Limera.[6] In a fragment from Athens recording the improvements made by one of the priests, occurs the word ἐφύτευσε, which shows the care taken of the sacred grove there.[7] In two reliefs from Athens,[8] which represent a sacrifice to Asklepios, Hygieia rests her hand on a large tree which seems to grow in the very temple. If these reliefs represent actual scenes, this implies that there was a sacred tree like the olive of the Erechtheum planted within the sanctuary. In the case of certain gods, trees are used either as images, or as symbols of the divinity. Such trees are hung with the attributes of the god. A laurel, hung with a quiver and bow, is sacred to Artemis, and a draped and crowned tree represent Dionysos. If the trees of the two Asklepios reliefs are to have a similar significance, they should bear the attributes of Asklepios. One of them, in fact, has the coils of a serpent about it.[9]

---

[1] Paus. II. 27, 1.

[2] δένδρη τὰ ἐν τῶι ἱαρῶι. Bau. 59, 121. An inquisitive man, Aeschines by name, once climbed into one of these trees and peeped over the wall into the sleeping-apartment of the suppliants. He met his punishment by falling out of the tree on some stakes which put out his eyes. Bau. 59, 90.

[3] Dion Cass. 51.　　　　　　　　　[4] Hippocr. ep. 13. (Kühn, p. 778.)
[5] Paus. II. 11, 6.　　　　　　　　　[6] Paus. III. 23, 7.
[7] Köhler, *ibid.* p. 241, and note.　　[8] BCH. 1878, pl. VII. and VIII.

[9] An unpublished relief now in the Glyptothek in München (85 a), said to have been found in Korinth, but more probably of Athenian origin, is referred by Professor Brunn to the cult of Asklepios on account of the general attitude of the divinities. The relief does bear a certain superficial resemblance to those from the Asklepieion in Athens. An elderly god is seated at the right, while before him stands a maiden in long garments. Before these figures is an altar, while a number of suppliants approach from the left bringing offerings, among which perhaps is a cock. Behind this group stands a large tree, hung with fillets, with sharply defined outlines. A column supports two small cult-statues, and a curtain is suspended from the boughs of the tree and completely fills the background. This tree is the only sure evidence we have of the use of sacred trees in the cult of Asklepios, unless we consider the two reliefs from Athens as conclusive. There is, however, considerable doubt whether the München relief should

In Tithorea buildings were erected in the enclosure for
the use of the attendants of the god and the patients.[1] In
Epidauros, however, the erection of permanent dwellings
within the precinct was at first forbidden, and only tents
could be used by the sick, the priests and by those who
came to assist at the festivals. The kind of tent to be used
in the festivals was regulated by law, that there might be no
inconvenience nor opportunity for thieving. The regulations
which are found in the ritual inscription of Andania[2] of the
second century B.C., probably apply to the festivals of Asklepios as well as to others. The tents are not more than thirty
feet long, and are not to be screened either by hides or doors.
They may contain no couches and no silver beyond the value
of three hundred drachmas. A patron of the sanctuary at
Delphi was allowed by the Amphictyons to have a tent in a
prominent place.[3] A part of the enclosure is marked off by
the priests, within which no one but themselves may have a
tent, and which only the initiates may enter. The custom of
bringing one's own tent to the Asklepieion in Epidauros lasted
until after the time of Hadrian, when Antoninus erected the first
permanent buildings for the use of women in child-birth and
the dying, as previously only roofless shelters were provided for
such.[4] An inscription of this time refers to the buildings of
the priests, still calling them σκανά out of respect for tradition.[5] As Pausanias mentions that women neither died nor
gave birth within the boundary wall, a fact which is confirmed

---

be referred to Asklepios. The winged beast which supports the chair is unlike
any representations we know; Asklepios and Hygieia both carry sceptres of
peculiar pattern, and any definite attribute is wanting. Moreover, the general
style of the relief has occasioned some doubts of its genuineness, though
Professor Brunn is sure of its authenticity.

[1] Paus. X. 32, 12.   [2] Le Bas, II. 326 a.
[3] Le Bas, II. 841, l. 11.   [4] Paus. II. 27, 6.
[5] Coll. 3359.   Θεός, ἀγαθὰ τύχα
Σκανὰ ἱερέων κ[αὶ]
Διονυσίου νακόρου
Θεο]χάριδος πυροφόρου.

by the steles, the buildings of Antoninus were most probably
not within the precinct, but immediately outside. Similar
buildings were put up in the precinct of Amphiaraos in
Oropos, where remains of them are still to be seen. An
inscription marks the precinct line and contains a decree
that no private citizen shall erect a permanent building within
it.[1] Open porticoes were in many Asklepieia for the use of
patients. In Epidauros there was a building of two stories,
and exercise was taken on the second.[2] The suppliants
sometimes used the portico as a sleeping-apartment, where
the god visited them as well as in the regular κοιμητήριον.[3]
The porticoes of Pergamon may have been either attached
to the temple or were separate buildings, for εἰς τὴν στοὰν
τοῦ ἱεροῦ πρὸς τῷ θεάτρῳ means either the side near the
theatre, or the one portico which was near it.[4]

The purifying and healing qualities of fresh water are so
well known, that it is hardly necessary to call attention to the
significance of the spring to be found in connection with
every Asklepieion. The fancy which peopled the trees and
mountains with good spirits, gave to each spring its guardian
nymph. Springs often had oracular powers,[5] and some restored
the sick to health.[6] The cult of Asklepios may often have
been introduced where a well was held as sacred, and the
nymph subordinated to the new god, accounting for the
presence of minor divinities which figure as daughters of
Asklepios. The stone found at the spring at Athens bears
the words "the boundary of the well,"[7] dating from the
second half of the fifth century. As the stone marked the

---

[1] BCH. III. p. 437.   ὅρος. Μὴ τοιχοδομεῖν
ἐντὸς τῶν ὅρων ἰδιώ
την.

[2] περιπάτῳ χρῆσθαι ὑπερῴῳ. Bau. 60, 10. Cf. Antyllus in Oribas I. 508. οἱ δὲ
ὑπερῷοι πάντων περιπάτων προκριτέοι.

[3] Bau. 80, 11.   [4] Aristid. 506, 2.

[5] Plut. Arist. XI. Paus. VII. 21, 12.   [6] Paus. V. 5, 11; VI. 22, 7.

[7] Mitth. d. Arch. Inst. II. p. 183.

boundary of the precinct of Asklepios, it more naturally would have borne an inscription to that effect if the well had not been held in greater reverence as the seat of a cult before the introduction of Asklepios. There is a tradition that at the well of Asklepios, Alkippe, the daughter of Ares and Aglauros, was attacked by Halirrhothios, a son of Poseidon.[1] This is a legend to account for the brackish taste of the water. Alkippe has been supposed to be a fountain nymph who was replaced by Hygieia at the introduction of the Asklepios cult. But Hygieia was not brought from Epidauros, and during the first fifty years of the cult in Athens was not known at all. Aristides supposed that nymphs have charge of the fountain of Asklepios and are to be greeted by the suppliants.[2]

The fountains were enclosed in more or less elaborately decorated buildings. The one at Epidauros was particularly beautiful.[3] There was a second supply of water near the great statue of the god, for when Pausanias was curious to know why the priests used neither oil nor water upon the image, while in Olympia and Athens similarly fashioned statues required one or the other, he was told that the statue of the god and his seat were near the well, ἐπὶ φρέατι.[4] The well-house in Athens was closed by doors, and an entrance of some sort led to it.[5] The spring of Amphiaraos in Oropos was not used for sacrificing or purification, but if a disease was cured at the shrine, a gold or silver coin was thrown into it.[6] The well at Pergamon, to quote Aristides, was in the most beautiful spot of the whole earth. " The part of the temple which is open to the air and accessible, βάσιμος, is in a very lovely spot, in the very middle of which is the well. The water flows from a plane-tree, or, if you prefer, from the very foundation of the temple itself, which is a more beautiful and holy thought. So every

---

[1] Paus. I. 21, 4.   [2] Aristid. 469, 2.
[3] Paus. II. 27, 5.   [4] Paus. V. 11, 11.
[5] Σωκράτης Σαραπίωνος Κηφισ[ιεὺς Ἀσκ]ληπιῶι καὶ Ὑγι[είαι] τὴν κρήνην καὶ τὴν εἴσοδο[ν · · ·] ἐν καὶ ἐθύρωσεν. Ἀθήν. V. 527, 10.
[6] Paus. I. 34, 4.

one believes that the water flows from a wholesome and
beneficial place, as it proceeds from the temple and the very
feet of the Saviour God." [1]   The latter part of the oration
about the well contains extravagant praise of the qualities
of the water.   Aristides declares that between a glass of it,
and a glass of sweetest wine, he would choose the former.
In connection with the springs, houses for baths were provided, and in the later centuries there was extensive use
of them in the cures.   Even a hasty reading of Aristides
gives an impression of a series of hot and cold baths, varied
by baths in the neighboring river or sea.   He says he cannot
enumerate the number of times, or the rivers, springs or seas
where he was ordered by the god to bathe, in Elaea, Smyrna,
and in other places.[2]

Within the walls of the τέμενος were altars to Asklepios, and
to any of the other gods found in connection with him.   The
character of Asklepios makes it probable that the first form of
altar was such as is found with the Chthonian deities and
heroes.   These altars were roughly hewn stones with a hole
through which the blood of sacrifices or wine might run to
be absorbed into the earth.   "The Chthonian gods welcome
the holes in the ground, and sacrifices in the hollows of the
earth." [3]   Köhler found at Athens what he thinks may have
been a hole used for such sacrifices to Asklepios.   Such altars
are called ἐσχάραι, but I have found no instance of the word in
connection with Asklepios, in whose cult βωμοί, or high altars
are used.[4]   A number of altars were placed outside the main
temple in Epidauros [5] and were made as offerings to the god.[6]
One altar could serve for several gods, ὁμόβωμοι.[7]   Pausanias
made no distinction between βωμοί and ἐσχάραι, for the βωμός
of the Samian Hera, he says, is no more beautiful than what

---

[1] Aristid. 410.   [2] Aristid. 486, 13.
[3] Philost. Vit. Apoll. VI. 11, p. 115.   [4] Mitth. d. Arch. Inst. II. 254.
[5] Bau. 43; 68; 84, 28, 31; Le Bas, II. 146 a.   [6] CIA. II. 3, 1650.
[7] CIA. II. 3, 1442.   Girard, L'Ascl. Appendix.

the Athenians call *extemporary altars*, ἐσχάραι αὐτοσχέδιοι.[1] So his use of the word βωμός may be an inaccuracy, and not imply that Asklepios had no ἐσχάραι.[2] The altars were usually round, or oblong, if high, but were also triangular in shape, τρίβωμος.[3] At Pergamon, a preliminary sacrifice was made after digging a trench outside the Hieron.[4]

The cave, which was the original place of worship, was superseded by the ordinary temple, in the classical period, and only traces remain of the former usage ; Trophonios, however, kept his early character. The account which Pausanias gives of Trophonios at Lebadeia, is a fair picture of the early ritual of Asklepios. "The oracle is above the grove on the mountain. And around it is a circular wall of stone, the circumference of which is very small, and the height of which rather less than two cubits. And there are some brazen pillars with connecting girders, and between them are doors. Inside is a cavity in the earth, not natural, but artificial, and built with great skill. The shape of this cavity resembles that of an oven. There are no steps to the bottom ; but when one descends to Trophonios, they furnish him with a narrow and light ladder. On the descent between top and bottom is an opening, two spans broad and one high. He that descends lies flat at the bottom of the cavity, and, having in his hands cakes kneaded with honey, introduces into the opening first his feet and then his knees ; and then all his body is sucked in, as a rapid and large river swallows up any one who is sucked into its vortex."[5] In this place Pausanias used the word ἄδυτον, which is the term used in the Asklepieia.[6] In the Pæan of Isyllos, it is said that one would not *go down* into the shrine of Asklepios in Trikka in Thessaly unless he had just sacrificed at the altar

---

[1] Paus. V. 13, 8.

[2] A relief representing suppliants with dish and pitcher has on the ground a round object which may be the ἐσχάρα; as it is too flat for the omphalos. Löwy, Zwei Reliefs der Villa Albani. Jahrb. d. kais. deut. Arch. Inst. II. 107.

[3] CIG. 5980.

[4] ἐπιβόθρια. Aristid. 472, 11.

[5] Paus. IX. 39, 9 ff.

[6] Bau. 84, 30.

of Apollo Maleatas. The words εἰς ἄδυτον καταβάς tell the
whole story of the cave which was in the temple, a remnant of
the primitive ritual.   Once the word ἄδυτον is used on the
steles from Epidauros, when a paralytic was carried out of the
ἄδυτον.[1] This may be a slip for ἄβατον, the usual name for the
sleeping room, or it may go to prove that the *sanctum sanc-
torum* was the very place where the cures were made.   For
in most temples there were certain regulations about the
entrances into the inner shrine, and only the priests or especially purified persons could enter.   A long set of rules required
the priest of Amphiaraos to be in the Hieron at least ten
days in each of the winter months, not leaving an interval of
more than three days.[2]   In Sikyon there was a double building,
and Apollo Karneios had the inner shrine, which only the
priests might enter.[3]

The temple, ναός or σηκός, was never an imposing structure.
The Athenian temple is called ἀφίδρυμα,[4] a model, and is
probably a copy of the Epidaurian temple.   The shrine at
Gerenia was an ἀφίδρυμα of the temple of Asklepios at Trikka.[5]
The temple had a vestibule, πρόνηος, formed by the prolonga-
tion of the sides, in which some of the offerings were kept.
Here Aristides offered a prayer before entering the temple.[6]
The προπύλαια of the temple of Pergamon were porticoes, and
were either the enclosed part in front, or they extended
entirely around it.[7]   Herodotus used the word in the latter
sense.[8]   In Athens the πρόπυλον was a covered vestibule.[9]
The word does not occur in the Epidaurian inscriptions.

The temple was locked at night, but at Pergamon a single
entrance was left so that the interior was seen.[10]   If the latticed

---

[1] Bau. 80, 112.

[2] Ἐφ. ἀρχ. 1885, 94.   Hermes, XXI. p. 91, l. 3.

[3] Paus. II. 10, 2.

[4] CIA. II. 1, Add. et Corr. 489 b.

[5] Strab. VIII. 4, 4.

[6] Aristid. 449, 13.

[7] Aristid. 447, 19; 473, 18.

[8] Hdt. II. 63, 101, 121, etc.

[9] CIA. II. 1, Add. et Corr. 489 b.   Köhler, Mitth. d. Arch. Inst. II. p. 174.

[10] καὶ τυχεῖν ἐν τούτῳ κλεισθὲν τὸ ἱερὸν οὕτω μέντοι ὥστε καὶ συγκεκλεισμένου εἰσοδόν
τέ τινα λείπεσθαι καὶ τὰ ἔνδον ὁρᾶσθαι.   Aristid. 448, 1.

gate, κιγκλίς,[1] is the temple door, there was a glimpse of the valuables through it.   The key was sacred, and the key-keepers had no unimportant office.   A coin of the second century B.C., from Pergamon, bears on the obverse a bearded head of Asklepios, and on the reverse a serpent and key.[2]

Within the temple were the statues of Asklepios and of any other gods worshipped with him.   Before the image was an altar or table for offerings, whose decoration was the care of the priest.[3]   At Pergamon a three-legged table stood at the right of the god, with three golden images, one at each foot, of Asklepios, Hygieia, and Telesphoros,[4] and in Syracuse the table was of gold.[5]   Near by was a couch on which at public festivals the statue of Asklepios was laid for the sacred repast. Here hung the offerings brought from time to time by the worshippers.   The heavy reliefs, however, were placed outside, either on pedestals, or fixed on the inner wall of the περίβολος, like the steles of Epidauros.[6]   The treasury was behind the image in the ναός.[7]

There was little uniformity in the various Asklepieia in regard to the place for sleeping.   As has been already mentioned, the suppliants may sleep in the porticoes, or in the presence of the cult-images, in an ante-room, or an especial apartment was provided.   In the sanctuary of Amphiaraos the sleepers find place about the altar, the men on the east, and the women on the west.[8]   Such was the accommodation at the smaller Asklepieia.   Aristophanes describes a single room at Athens containing an altar for the preliminary sacrifices and

---

[1] Arist. Vesp. 125.   Aristid. 484, 1.

[2] W. Wroth.   Num. Chron. 1882, I. p. 17.   "On fictile vases the key is a usual attribute of priestesses, and, with regard to the likelihood of such temple keys appearing on coins, we may mention that Dr. Imhoof-Blumer claims to have found the sacred key of the sanctuary of Argive Hera on the reverse of a silver coin of Argos which has the head of the goddess on the other side."

[3] τὴν τράπεζαν ἐκόσμησεν καλῶς καὶ φιλοτίμως.   CIA. II. 1, Add. et Corr. 373 b. See the reliefs from Athens.

[4] Aristid. 516, 15.   Cf. 495, 23.   [5] Athenae. XV. 693, 2.

[6] Paus. II. 27, 3.   [7] Bau. 87, 12.   [8] Hermes, XXI. p. 93.

couches for the sleepers.   This was separate from the shrine,
for the serpents enter the sleeping apartment from the latter,
and return into it.[1]   Here stood a table on which the offerings
were laid, not, however, for the formal sacrifices to the god.[2]
It is perhaps such a room which Suidas called πρόδομος, where
a cure took place.[3]   In Epidauros a special room was built for
the sleepers beyond the temple.[4]   This was called ἄβατον[5] or
ἐγκοιμητήριον.[6]   The form κοιμητήριον is used in Oropos.[7]

A number of lamps were lighted in the sleeping room each
evening, under the supervision of the priest.   Aristides says
" it was after the hour of the sacred lamps,"[8] and " at one
time he asked an attendant where the priest was, and he was
told that he was behind the temple, for he was seeing about
lighting the lamps."[9]   The lights were extinguished when the
suppliants were ready for the night.[10]

---

[1] Arist. Plut. 652–747.   ἐκ τοῦ νεώ, l. 733.

 εἰς τὸν νεών, l. 746.

[2] εἰσὶ γὰρ τράπεζαι ἐν τοῖς ἱεροῖς ἐν αἷς τιθέασι τὰ ἐπιφερόμενα.   Sch. Arist. Plut. 678.

[3] Suid. art. Δομνῖνος.   [4] Paus. II. 27, 2.

[5] Bau. 59, 4, 21, 50, 63, 65, 91, 109, 116, 117; 60, 19; 80, 23, 25, 44, 49, 51, 102.

[6] Bau. 61, 7.   [7] Hermes, XXI. p. 93, l. 43.

[8] Aristid. 541, 11.   [9] Aristid. 447, 28.   [10] Arist. Plut. 668.

CHAPTER IV.

ATTENDANTS OF THE TEMPLE.

THE priest was responsible for the correct administration of the ritual. He was in charge of the buildings first of all, seeing each day that they were in order and ready for the services.[1] The decoration of the temple and other preparations for sacrifice were his duty.[2] In short, all the service of the day was in his care.[3] He officiated at sacrifices, receiving and caring for the offerings of the suppliants.[4] Of these gifts he kept a strict account and reported any loss or injury. Certain gifts have become old;[5] three drachmas have been lost.[6] Some valuables the priest kept at his own house for safety.[7] At the close of his term of office the priest formally made over to his successor whatever had accumulated during his administration. Examples of such inventories of the temple - valuables have been found at Athens.[8] Decrees authorized the appointment of commis-

---

[1] Coll. 3052. [· · · κοσμεῖ]ν δὲ τὸν ἱερῆ τὸν ναὸν κατ' ἀμέ[ραν · ἐπιμέ]λεσθαι δὲ αὐτὸν καὶ τᾶς στοιᾶ[ς τᾶς πο]ττῶι 'Ασκλαπιείωι ὅπως καθαρ[ὰ ἦι] · · ·. Cf. Hermes, XVI. p. 164 ff.

[2] CIA. II. 1, Add. Nov. 477 b. ἐπιμεμέληται δὲ καὶ τῆς [τοῦ να]οῦ εὐκοσμίας 'Αθήν. VI. p. 134, n. 9. [ἐπιμελεῖται?] τῆς εὐκοσμίας τῆς περ[ὶ τὸ ἱερόν] CIA. II. 1, Add. et Corr. 453 b and c. ἔστρωσεν δὲ καὶ τὰς κλ[ίνας · · ·]

[3] CIA. II. 1, Add. et Corr. 453 b. [τὰς κα]θ' ἑκάστην ἡμέραν γινομένας θε[ραπείας · · ·] Cf. Girard, L'Ascl. p. 26.

[4] Arist. Plut. 676.

[5] CIA. II. 2, 766, l. 7. Μύννιον Γ· ταύτας ἔφη ὁ ἱερε[ὺς] Εὐνικίδης 'Αλαιεὺς παλαιὰς εἶναι.

[6] Ibid. l. 2. Μνησαρέτη Δ, ἐλλείπει ΗΗ, ταύτας δεῖ[ν] ἔφη ἀποδοῦναι Διοκλέα Μυῤῥι(νούσιον).

[7] CIA. II. 2, 835, l. 62. τάδε ἐστὶν ἀργυρᾶ παρὰ τῷ ἱερεῖ · · ·.

[8] CIA. II. 2, 835, 836 and 839. The inventories differ in arrangement. In the first the position of each object in the temple is given, while in the second the offerings and their donors are grouped according to the date of the sacrifice.

sioners who, with the priest of Asklepios and two other
officers, were to choose out of the offerings a certain number
to be placed in the temple.	The number of offerings increased
so rapidly that such a removal was occasionally necessary.

- At the expiration of his office the priest came forward in
the Boulê and reported upon the sacrifices which according
to law he had offered in behalf of the state.[1]	If the report
was satisfactory, a decree of thanks was voted.	The decree
was set in the Asklepieion and a crown of gold or olive given
the priest.[2]	Other more substantial perquisites belonged to
the office.	A seat in the theatre of Dionysos still bears his
name.[3]	In many places he was allowed to live within the
precincts and have use of whatever land about the temple
was not already occupied by the city.[4]	In Mantineia there
was a college of priests, who lived together sharing the meals
of the day.	The income for their support seems to have come
from the bounty of the suppliants, for an offering of grapes
was given, not to the god, but directly to them.	For this
service the donor received an image in the temple, and on her
birthday the priests made a special sacrifice in her behalf.[5]
If the services of the priest were not required constantly, he
could reside where he pleased, and come only occasionally to
the temple, as in the case of the priest of Amphiaraos.[6]	He
might wear a crown at the festivals and enjoy the public
banquets.[7]	Part of the sacrifices were given to him.[8]

The priest offers sacrifices in his own behalf and dedicates
tablets to Asklepios and other gods of the same sanctuary.

For example, line 77 of the first is, · · · πρὸ]s τῷ τοίχῳ ὀφθαλμοὶ καὶ a[ἰδοῖ]ον,
ἃ ἀνέθηκ[εν] Σωτηρίδηs · ὦτα IIII, ἃ ἀνέθηκε Βοΐδαs · ἐν δεξιᾶ[ι] τοῦ θεοῦ σφ[η · · ·.
Line 18 of the second, [θέντα ἐφ' ἱερέωs Λυσικλ]έου[s] Συπαληττ(ίου) · χεὶρ
[Π]ρομένου · · ·.

[1] CIA. II. 1, Add. Nov. 477 b.	[πρ]όσοδον ποιησάμενος πρὸs τὴμ βουλὴν ἀπήγγελ[λ]εν
[2] CIA. II. 1, Add. Nov. 373 b; 477 b and c; 567 b.	Similar decrees were
voted in other cults.	Cf. CIA. II. 1, 453; 457.
[3] CIA. III. 1, 263; 287.	[4] Coll. 3052.
[5] Le Bas-Foucart, 352 j.	Immerwahr, Die Kulte u. Mythen Arkadiens, p. 176 ff.
[6] Hermes, XXI. p. 91, 1-6.	[7] Coll. 3052.	[8] See Chapter VII. p. 80.

In Epidauros, Diogenes, who was not only a priest but an hierophant [1] and propole of Zeus, dedicates to Zeus and Helios a tablet of some length,[2] and shorter ones to Apollo, Selene, Telesphoros, Hygieia, Apollo Maleatas and Asklepios.[3]

Historically considered, a priest was such from his position at the head of his family. In the worship of the family gods, the duties of sacrifice and prayer devolved upon the oldest son. As the family became the tribe, its head kept the priestly duties, and if the cult grew to be a state religion, the king or a priest appointed by the state took charge of it. This, then, was the starting point; a family cult, with a priest whose only special knowledge was of correct ritual, needing no teacher but observation, no theology but intuition. Such a priesthood was hereditary and the office was for life. When a new cult was introduced into a family, the same would hold good; the founder of a cult became its minister, and transmitted the ritual to his sons. This primitive method survived in some of the temples of Asklepios. In Pergamon the office passed from father to son.[4] An inscription from Lebena, which is a prayer to Asklepios for additional water facilities in the temple, alludes to a miraculous disclosure to Aristonymos at some former time, and prayer is made for a similar miracle for the present priest, Soarchos, son of Agagas, who is now in the forty-seventh year of his office. Agagas had also been a priest of Asklepios, and his son had assumed his duties under the title of τίτας πατέρος, a legal term in use in Gortyna for one who assumes responsibility for another.[5] It is scarcely to be doubted that here, too, the priesthood was hereditary. Such was also the case in Lesbos.[6]

---

[1] Another priest was also a Hierophant. Bau. 62. [2] Bau. 1.

[3] Bau. 37–42. Cf. Bau. 24; 47; 53; 57; 57 a; 58; 62; 63; 67; 68; 97. CIA. III. 1, Add. et Corr. 102 a, b and c. CIG. 1177; 1178.

[4] Aristid. 521, 11. ταύτῃ μοι ἐδόκει ὁ ἱερεὺς ὁ τοῦ Ἀσκληπιοῦ οὗτος ὁ ἔτι νῦν ὢν καὶ ὁ τούτου πάππος, ἐφ' οὗ τὰ πολλὰ καὶ μεγάλα ὡς ἐπυνθανόμεθα ἐχειρούργησεν ὁ θεὸς καὶ · · ·. [5] Philol. 1890, p. 583.

[6] Coll. 260. ἱρευς διὰ γένεος τῷ Σωτῆρος Ἀσκληπίω καὶ ἱρευς διὰ βίω Λεσβίοις.

Evidence of the purchase of priesthood is found in an inscription of about 200 B.C., from Chalkedon.[1] Any one who is eligible for public office, sound in mind and body, may buy the priesthood for himself or his son. The purchaser shall pay in two installments, after the second of which he is consecrated. Whatever expense is incurred during this ceremony is defrayed by the priest. If any one disputes his claim, he renders himself liable to a fine of a thousand drachmas to be paid to the treasury of Asklepios. The price of the priesthood shall be about five thousand drachmas with an added tax.

In Athens, the cult was on a very different basis. The control which the state assumed over the political life of its members was extended to include the religious life. For to the Greek, religion was not a personal matter. He had no religious opinions. Religion consisted merely of an observance of certain traditional usages which was the only expression of the relation of suppliant and divinity. The state had every right to interfere and to prescribe that for its safety a certain ritual be performed. If a neglect of proper sacrifice and prayer could bring calamity in form of pestilence or war, the city must take precautions against such disaster, and cults came to be a vital part of the public life. Hence numerous decrees in Athens relate to the Asklepios cult. In the fourth century, the cult was entirely under the control of the state. A priest who wishes to repair and restore parts of the temple at his own expense petitions the state, and the Boulê gravely permits him to do so.[2] The order of ritual is prescribed by the state. A priest is praised for his zeal in performing certain political duties which devolve upon him

---

[1] Coll. 3052. See Dittenberger in Hermes, XVI. p. 164 ff. The sale of the office, though occurring but once in the cult of Asklepios, was not uncommon in other cults. A thorough investigation of this usage in Erythrae has been made by Dr. Gaebler, *Erythrae. Untersuchungen über die Geschichte u. die Verfassung der Stadt im Zeitalter des Hellenismus.* Berlin, 1892.

[2] CIA. II. 1, Add. et Corr. 489 *b.*

by the law.[1]   So we are not surprised to find that the priests
were chosen as any other official of the state, by lot, annually.
For one as well as another can perform the sacrifice, repeat
the prayers and chant the pæans.   A knowledge of correct
ritual was the only requisite for the office.   Heretical opinions
were unknown.   We have clear evidence of the choice by lot
in Athens,[2] while the length of the term of office, namely,
one year, points to the same method of choice.[3] Besides the
direct limitation of the length of office, the decrees relating
to the cult were dated by the name of the priest, ἐπὶ ἱερέως,
or without the preposition,[4] and in Epidauros with ἔτους.[5]

The lots were cast some time before the priest came into
office.   Diokles, who petitioned for the right to repair the
temple, did so in the archonship of Lysander, and entered
upon his duties in the archonship of Lysiades.   The statements of Mr. Headlam, about this method of appointing
religious officials, in a recent essay on election by lot, are at
variance with what I have assumed in regard to the development of a cult.   According to him, the lot is a method of
learning the will of the gods, which made it peculiarly fitting
for the election of a priest that "the God himself should
choose those who were to serve him. . . .   This custom prevailed till the latest times, and though it had probably become
a mere ritual observance, it is at least a sign that the appointment of a priest had not the highest validity unless it had
received the express sanction of the God.   It is easy, then,
to assume that the lot which was so essential a part of the

---

[1] CIA. II. 1, Add. Nov. 477 b.   κατὰ [τὰ] ψηφίσματα.   CIA. II. 1, Add. Nov.
567 b.   ἐπιμελεῖται δὲ καὶ τῆς κληρώσεως τῶν δικασ[τη]ρίων καὶ τῶν ἄλλων ὧν αὐτῷ οἱ
τ[ε] νόμοι καὶ τὰ ψηφίσματα προστάττουσιν δικαίως καὶ κατὰ το(ὺ)ς νόμους · · ·.

[2] CIA. II. 1, Add. Nov. 567 b.   Φυλεὺς λαχὼν ἱερεὺς τοῦ Ἀσκ. · · ·   CIA. II. 1,
Add. et Corr. 489 b.   ὁ εἰληχὼς ἱερεὺς Ἀσκληπιοῦ · · ·   CIA. II. 1, Add. Nov.
352 b.   τὸν [ἱερέα τὸν ἀεὶ λα]νχάνοντ[α · · ·

[3] CIA. II. 1, Add. et Corr. 453 b.   Φλυεὺς ὁ γενόμε[νος ἱερεὺς Ἀσκληπιοῦ καὶ
Ὑγιείας ἐπὶ] τὸν ἐπὶ Τιμάρχου ἄρχοντος ἐ[νιαυτόν.

[4] CIA. III. 1, 693.

[5] Bau. 6 a and b; 61, 17.

religious ceremonial, retained its religious significance when used for political purposes ; and even to draw the conclusion that the religious belief was really the chief reason why it was so extensively used." [1]

I should myself be willing to believe that the use of the lot in political affairs was a survival of a time when the gods were believed to exercise control over affairs of the state, and that the casting came to be a meaningless observance, but in view of the original tribal element in Greek cults, it seems hardly possible that such was the primitive method of priest selection.   It is only at Athens that the system was in vogue. Mr. Headlam himself instances examples enough to show that in the fifth century nearly all religious feeling was lost in the ceremony.   So when we find the priests of Asklepios chosen annually by lot, we must recognize that the cult has come under the jurisdiction of the state, and that the usage of state officials has been introduced and has supplanted an earlier system.

There is an exception to the general rule of choice by lot, which is found in an inscription of the time of Demosthenes.[2] Demon, a relative of Demosthenes,[3] was by oracle commanded to give his house and orchard to Asklepios, and to become priest.

In Kos, the priests were yearly appointed from one of the tribes κατὰ θείαν κέλευσιν, an ambiguous expression which may imply the use either of lot or direct oracle.[4]   It is more probable that the former prevailed.   The limitation of the choice to a single family suggests that the science of medicine was at this time confined to a fraternity.

During the later years of the cult, a second priest held office for life.[5]   There were also priests for life in Kos,[6] Stratonikeia in Karia,[7] and Thera.[8]

---

[1] Election by Lot at Athens.   James Wycliffe Headlam.   Cambridge, 1891. Introd. pp. 5-6.   [2] CIA. II. 3, 1654.
[3] Plut. Demosth. XXVII.   [4] Paton and Hicks, Inscr. of Cos. No. 103.
[5] CIA. III. 1, 132; Add. et Corr. 68 *a* and *b* ; 229 *a*.
[6] BCH. V. p. 474.   [7] BCH. XII. p. 88.
[8] Ross. Inscr. Ined. II. 221.

From the Epidaurian inscriptions there is little to throw light on the selection of priests. The term of office was one year, if we may judge from the dating of a few inscriptions by the name of the priest.[1] Foucart suggests that the Σκανά in use in Epidauros were intended for the priests of the different temples within the enclosure, and as they were annually chosen, their names were not given, while the νακόρος and the πυρφόρος are mentioned by name, as they held office for life.

The attendant who is most frequently mentioned in connection with the Asklepieia is the νεωκόρος, or ζάκορος, the form used at Athens and in an inscription from Bresos.[2]

The care of the property of the god devolved upon him, subject, always, to the supervision of the priest.[3] In Oropos the priest compelled him, according to law, to care for the sanctuary and those who come into it. He inscribed the names of the suppliants and their homes upon a post in the temple, and took charge of the deposit of offerings.[4] The neocore was in fact the representative of the priest. He helped to arrange the images, and otherwise make preparation for the sacrifices.[5] From Crete we have directions for the surrender of duties on the expiration of office. Here the neocore was responsible for the utensils and treasury of the temple.[6] Sometimes he had charge of the keys, which were usually entrusted to special officials.[7] The neocore might take the place of the priest also in the administration of ritual. In Kos he declared the omens and offered prayer to the god for the suppliants.[8] In Pergamon there were two

---

[1] Bau. 6 *a* and *b*; 60; 61. Coll. 3025.

[2] Coll. 255.

[3] The word νεωκόρος has usually been interpreted as temple-sweeper. Et. Mag. ὁ τὸν ναὸν κοσμῶν καὶ σαρῶν. Suidas, however, contradicts this. Νεωκόρος δὲ οὐχ ὁ σαρῶν τὸν νεών, ἀλλ' ὁ ἐπιμελούμενος αὐτοῦ.

[4] Hermes, XXI. p. 92.

[5] CIA. III. 1, Add. et Corr. 68 *c*. · · · ζακορεύων τὰ ζῴδια ἐπεσκεύασα καὶ τὴν τράπεζαν.

[6] Philol. 1890, p. 587, l. 6.   [7] Aristid. 447, 29.

[8] Herond. IV. ll. 40; 45; 90.

neocores who interpreted dreams and took active part in the services.[1] In Epidauros was but one neocore for the whole precinct, though it included several temples. The office was, as has been shown, for life.

In Athens the ζάκορος was of great importance, for his name was used with that of the priest and archon to date many inscriptions relating to the cult, which shows that he, too, held office but for a year.[2] He was appointed as the priest was, and like his superior officer, dedicated tablets after his work was done.[3] In one case he laid at his own expense, and dedicated to Asklepios and Hygieia, the flooring in the vestibule and about the altar.[4] Diaphantos left a long and elaborate prayer for help, and a thank-offering for recovery from illness.[5] Sometimes the ζάκορος was a physician, and a decree was voted in his honor.[6] There was an assistant zacore at Athens, chosen and holding office in the same way as the zacore.[7]

There is also a third name, πρόπολος, which is given to the attendant nearest the priest in importance. The chief source of information about him is the scene in Plutos, where he extinguishes the lights and tells the suppliants to sleep. The Scholiast writes that he is the νεωκόρος, but again that he is the ἱερεύς.[8] The second statement holds good in Epidauros, for Diogenes, who is a priest of Apollo, is a propole of Zeus.[9]

The importance of the key-keeper has already been mentioned. In Athens his name appears to determine the date of decrees.[10] There is no allusion to the office in Epidauros, nor at Pergamon, where the neocore has charge of the keys.

---

[1] Aristid. 473, 5; 474, 12; 494, 11.

[2] CIA. III. 1, Add. et Corr. 132 o; 181 c, f and h. See Index.

[3] CIA. III. 1, 102. See Index.

[4] CIA. III. 1, Add. et Corr. 68 e and f.   [5] CIA. III. 1, Add. et Corr. 171 a.

[6] CIA. III. 1, 780; Add. et Corr. 780 a, b and c.

[7] CIA. III. 1, Add. et Corr. 894 a.   [8] Sch. Arist. Plut. 670.

[9] Bau. 1, 10.

[10] CIA. III. 1, Add. et. Corr. 102 a; 780 a.

It is likely that the office of the κλειδοῦχος was extended in Athens in the same way as that of the νεωκόρος, and that its duties were ritualistic rather than actual, and existed separately only in Athens, where the ritual was most elaborate. It was the custom for the priest to appoint his son as key-keeper, which confirms this conclusion,[1] for his daughters were chosen by him to assist in the ceremony connected with the processions.[2]

The duty of lighting the altar-fire was important enough to necessitate the appointment of an officer called πυρφόρος. The office is frequently mentioned in Epidauros, though in the inscriptions the participle, πυρφορήσας, is used rather than the noun. The dedications by one who styles himself a fire-bearer furnish no clue to the duties of the office.[3] The parents of Menander dedicated their son to be a πυρφόρος in the service of Asklepios and Apollo.[4]

In some instances the duty of lighting the altar-fire was per-formed by young boys, who filled the office of incense-bearer. In one instance we know this was the case, ὁ παῖς ὁ τῶι θεῶι πυρφορῶν,[5] but the tense is not the usual one, and so the "boy" may be but a substitute for the regular attendant. Yet the present tense of the participle is regularly used in other cults, as in Laconian τὸν σὶν φέρων.[6] The πυρφόρος held office for life. There is but a single mention of the fire-bearer in Athens.[7] The μάγιρος took part in the service in Epidauros, and consecrated a stone to Asklepios.[8] An ἱεροκῆρυξ is men-

[1] CIA. II. 1, Add. et Corr. 453 b and c.
[2] CIA. II. 1, Add. et Corr. 453 b; II. 3, 1204; III. 1, Add. et Corr. 920 a.
[3] Bau. 5; 6 a and b; 55; 69; 72. CIG. 1178.
[4] Bau. 49. I am led to this conclusion by the employment of the genitive case of the name of the god with πυροφορήσας in other inscriptions instead of the more logical dative, an example of syntactical "contamination" borrowed from the phrase πυρφόρος Ἀσκληπιοῦ. The dative in this place is probably governed by some verb easily supplied, as ἀνατιθέναι, which is used for the consecration of a slave to Serapis and Isis in Orchomenos. BCH. IV. p. 91, l. 10.
[5] Bau. 59, 43.   [6] Cauer, 33, 51.
[7] CIA. III. 1, 693. Ἀσκληπιοῦ με δμῶα πυρφόρο[ν, ξενε,] · · ·   [8] Bau. 101.

tioned in an Athenian inscription, but there is no evidence that the cult had a special officer of this sort.[1] An unusual title, ἰαρονγός, is found in Crete. There are but two attendants, the neocore, and this one, who takes the place of priest or head of the sanctuary.[2] The janitor, θυρωρός, at Pergamon, who brings in the lights, is one of the many minor attendants.[3]

A body of men lived at the temples who had nothing to do with the ritual, but assisted in the care of the patients. Aristides calls them πάντες οἱ περὶ τὸν θεὸν θεραπευταί.[4] They assist a man to a seat,[5] they follow the "god," and aid in surgical operations by holding the patient,[6] attempt operations themselves,[7] and carry a paralytic before the temple.[8] In the scene from the Plutos the surgeon is accompanied by two women, and a young boy brings a mortar and pestle.[9] There is little evidence of surgery at Athens, and the assistance of men is not required. Light duties about the temple were performed by boys who formed the choir.[10]

---

[1] CIA. III. 1, Add. et Corr. 780 *a*.

[2] Philol. 1890, p. 587, l. 5.   [3] Aristid. 433, 16.

[4] Aristid. 477, 15; 477, 26, καί τινα τῶν ὑπηρετῶν ἰδών · · ·.

[5] Bau. 59, 114.   [6] Bau. 80, 40.   [7] Bau. 80, 12.

[8] Bau. 80, 113.   [9] Arist. Plut. 710.   [10] Bau. 60, 19. Aristid. 470, 6.

CHAPTER V.

THE relation of priests to physicians in the temple is a point in dispute which can be determined only by a study of the cult in different localities and at different times. This will show a variety of usage; where the emphasis was ritualistic, the physician was subordinate to the priest and even wanting in some instances, but if the treatment of suppliants was at all scientific, the priest left the suppliant at the door of the sleeping-room, and a physician took the charge. In some places the cult was a worship of the god Asklepios, while in others, the temple became a hospital and the cult was subordinated. Such was the historical development of the whole institution also. For the worship of the god, a priest was necessary only for the purpose of conducting the sacrifices, offering prayers, and interpreting dreams. From the nature of the cures which were effected, we may judge whether there was any scientific handling of the cases. Attestations of the cures are of three kinds : first, the votive offerings left by patients, which represent the cured portion of the body ; second, the steles which tell the history of cures ; and last, a scanty collection of allusions in literature.

Votive offerings from Athens representing parts of the body are known to us through inventories.[1] These included almost every part of the body, besides representations of the entire person. The most common offering is a pair of eyes, gold or silver, showing that diseases of the eyes were even more prevalent in Greece than now. Aristophanes appropriately pictures the cure of a blind god. Some sort of truth must have been beneath the devotion which consecrated these

---

[1] CIA. II. 2, 766; 767; 835; 836; 839.

objects. Had the ritual been purely religious, these offerings would have been such as to please the deity, not to show
gratitude. But proof of a cure is no proof of its method. A
model of a man's hand may indicate a cure by miracle or
scientific treatment. As far as direct record goes, the cures
were effected by miracle only, as was supposed by the credulous. The existence of a great school of physicians at Athens
who sacrifice every year to Asklepios as their patron, points to
a lack of competition between sacred and secular practice.[1]
There may have been physicians in the Asklepieion, but their
presence is neither necessary nor can it be proved. The priest
was not a physician except in a few instances where after his
name the title ἰατρός is added as something unusual. The
same occurs in the case of the zacore several times. If these
offices had been hereditary, we can conceive that the priest and
physician might have been the same, and that medical skill as
well as knowledge of ritual might have been handed from
father to son. But both priest and zacore were chosen by lot,
nor is there any reason to suppose that they were taken from a
class of physicians. There is no proof that it was not so, but
the presumption is on the side of what is customary in other
cults. As far as any recorded cures in Athens go, there is
nothing to show anything more than the working of superstition upon the credulous. Although offerings are recorded
in a time of which we know much, among all the names of
suppliants not one is that of a well-known citizen. Does this
not suggest that the use of the oracle was confined to the more
ignorant classes, at least as a place of healing? For we must
not suppose that the cult had an inferior position in the
religious life of Athens. The balance of evidence leads one
to suppose that a well-informed citizen trusted in physicians
rather than gods, and let his physician pray and offer thanks
for his recovery. The cult in Athens was so entirely under
direction of law, that had there been an appointed physician

---

[1] CIA. II. 1, Add. Nov. 352 *b*; II. 3, 1449. Cf. CIG. 5974.

in the temple, we could scarcely have failed to know it. But beyond a doubt, the priest or zacore had *some* practical knowledge of medicine, and the amusing scene in the Plutos has much that is true in it. The nightly recurrence of the same malady must have given familiarity with it, and knowledge of its treatment. It would not have done for a sleeper to pass the night without a dream. So in the dim light, the priest and his attendants lay a hand on this one and that. The miracle comes to him who expects it. In the morning the dream is told, and wisely interpreted by the priest, a few simple directions are given, and the cure is effected.

A consideration of the Epidaurian steles shows a different state of affairs. There is, too, a variety of usage shown in the early records and those of the later days of the Roman Empire. The main evidence is given on two of the six steles which were in Epidauros in the time of Pausanias. These date from the third century before Christ. They bear the same formulas : — ἀμέρας δὲ γενομένας ὑγιὴς ἐξῆλθε · ἐκ τούτου ὑγιὴς ἐγένετο · καὶ ἐνύπνιον εἶδε. Usually the patient's name is in the nominative case with an adjective which describes the disease. The dialect is the Doric κοινή, and the style is uniformly simple. This uniformity points to a single hand in the records, either of a priest or an assistant. Similar steles were in Kos and Trikka,[1] but of these nothing has been found. It is said that Hippocrates learned much of the nature of disease and its remedies from the cures which were recorded in Kos.[2] Aristides is familiar with records left by suppliants.[3] In Epidauros the suppliants left tablets of their own,[4] and cure-steles were collections of temple traditions

---

[1] Strab. VIII. 6, 15. [2] Pliny, N. H. 29, 2.

[3] Aristid. 66, 9. καὶ καταλέγουσιν ἄλλος ἄλλο τι, οἱ μὲν ἀπὸ στόματος οὑτωσὶ φράζοντες, οἱ δὲ ἐν τοῖς ἀναθήμασιν ἐξηγούμενοι.

[4] Bau. 59, 7. τυχοῦσα δὲ τούτων ἐπὶ τὸ ἀνάθεμα ἐπεγράψατο ·
οὐ μέγεθος πίνακος θαυμαστέον, ἀλλὰ τὸ θεῖον,
πένθ᾽ ἔτη ὡς ἐκύησε ἐγ γαστρὶ Κλέω βάρος, ἔστε
ἐγκατεκοιμάθη, καί μιν ἔθηκε ὑγιῆ.

which until the third century were either transmitted verbally,
or recorded on the-slabs left by the patients.   Four methods
of cure were in use at this early date : surgery, use of drugs,
hypnotic treatment, and what may be called a miracle cure, in
cases for which no remedy is mentioned except the necessary
sleep in the temple.

If the surgical reports are at all true, it amounts to little less
than a miracle that the patients lived through the operations,
to say nothing of a cure being performed.   Surgery is the
most natural method, which goes farther back than the beliefs
in charms and incantations.   To cut off a part to save the
whole is the wholesome doctrine of an early and unreflecting
age.[1]   Burning and cutting were familiar to the thought of the
Greeks of the classical time.[2]   Aristogeiton was to be elimi-
nated from the state as physicians burn or cut a cancer or
other such plague from the body.[3]   Plato knows of four
means employed by physicians, and first in his mind come
burning and cutting.[4]   A large number of the cures at Epidauros are effected by surgery.   It is employed for an ulcer
in a case when the attendant of the god, that is, the surgeon,
had difficulty in holding the patient.   The floor covered with
blood proved the reality of the operation.[5]   Shrunken eyelids
were cut that a drug might be poured in.[6]   A soldier whose
eyesight was destroyed by a spear, the point of which he had
carried for a year in his face, had the spear removed and the
sight restored.[7]   Another spear point was taken from the jaw
of a patient,[8] and one from the lung of another.[9]   A Laconian
woman, Arata, was afflicted with dropsy.   As she was too ill

---

[1] Aristid. 472, 18.   δεῖν δὲ καὶ τοῦ σώματος αὐτοῦ παρατέμνειν ὑπὲρ σωτηρίας τοῦ
παντός.

[2] Aeschyl. Agam. 849.
ἤτοι κέαντες ἢ τεμόντες εὐφρόνως
πειρασόμεσθα πῆμ' ἀποστρέψαι νόσου.

[3] Demosth. 798, 95.   [4] Plato, Prot. 354 A.
[5] Bau. 80, 45.   [6] Bau. 59, 40.   [7] Bau. 80, 64.
[8] Bau. 59, 95.   [9] Bau. 80, 55.

to visit the sanctuary herself, her mother dreamed for her, and ·
had a vision of the god cutting off her daughter's head and‚
letting the water run from the neck. Then the god replaced
the head. On the mother's return, she found her daughter
cured, after having had the same vision.[1]

On the same stele is an account which gives more direct
evidence concerning the antiquity of the cult at Epidauros.
Aristagora of Troizen slept in the Asklepieion at that place,[2]
having a worm in the intestines. In her vision, the "sons
of the god" cut off her head, in the absence of the god who
was at Epidauros. As they were not able to replace the head,
they sent for Asklepios. In the meantime day appeared, and
the priest had a vision of the severed head. The next night
Aristagora saw a vision in which the god came from Epidauros
and put back her head, after which he cut out the worm
properly. And yet this absurd story ends with ἐκ τούτου ὑγιὴς
ἐγένετο. The same story is quoted by Aelian from Hippys
of Rhegion.[3] A woman had a worm, and the most skilled
physicians had abandoned her case as hopeless. So she came
to Epidauros and prayed for treatment. The god was not
there, but the ζάκοροι laid the woman where the god was
accustomed to treat the patients. ·She became quiet at their
command, and the attendants, ὑποδρῶντες τῷ θεῷ, did what
was necessary for the cure. They removed her head and
one put his hand into her body and drew out the worm,‚ a
monstrous beast. But they could not put back the head.
Then in came the god very angry at them for attempting
what was beyond their skill. With his divine power he
restored the head and raised the woman. Hippys lived in
the early part of the fifth century, Aelian in the second
century of our own era. The malpractice of the attendants

---

[1] Bau. 80, 1.

[2] This is the only evidence in literature that there was an Asklepieion in
Troizen, although a coin bears the standing figure of the god. Head, Hist.
Num., p. 371.

[3] Aelian, H. A. IX. 33.

of Troizen may have been introduced into the temple tradition in a spirit of rivalry between the two sanctuaries, and
the version of Hippys be the original form, or Hippys may
have chosen to ignore the real scene, and transfer the whole
to Epidauros. In either case, an early date is proved for
the cult at Epidauros.[1]

We may come to some definite conclusions about the attendants at Epidauros from these accounts. The hand of a skilled
surgeon was needed in important operations, while a number
of assistants were ready to undertake simple cures, and aid
the "god." The surgeon was not the priest, but there was
a double set of officers; the priest, neocore, and so forth,
and the surgeon and his assistants who are "sons of the
god," probably a clan in which medical knowledge is handed
from father to son.

Many of the cures were effected by use of drugs, φάρμακα,
whose nature cannot be determined. An eyelid was cut and
a drug poured in;[2] one man had no eyeballs at all, but an
application of the drug to the empty sockets restored the
sight.[3] We are reminded of the painful cure of Neokles in
Athens.[4] A preparation was known for the cure of baldness;[5]
an emetic was given.[6] There is nothing here to imply an
extensive knowledge of drugs, and so no proof for or against
the presence of a special physician.

A discussion of temple-sleep from the side of hypnotism
has been made by Dr. Carl du Prel.[7] The ground taken is
that the method of "temple-sleep" is the same as that in
use in producing a hypnotic state at the present day, and the
observed phenomena are the same. A cure is effected by
awakening a healing instinct in the sleeper himself. According to Dr. du Prel, the practice of temple-sleep was imported

---

[1] Wilamowitz, Hippys v. Rhegion, Hermes XIX. p. 442 ff. Zacher, Zu den
Heilurkunden v. Epid., Hermes XXI. p. 467 ff.

[2] Bau. 59, 40; 80, 121.   [3] Bau. 59, 77.   [4] Arist. Plut. 716.

[5] Bau. 59, 124.   [6] Bau. 80, 125.

[7] Dr. Carl du Prel, Die Mystik d. alten Griechen. Leipzig, 1888.

from Egypt.   The system of incubation in the temples of
Isis as described by Diodorus Siculus,[1] and of Serapis according to Strabo,[2] is similar to that in the Greek temples.   But
shall we on this account believe that the whole system was
an Egyptian product ?   The dream-oracle is sufficiently natural
and ancient to antedate the introduction of Egyptian deities
into Greece.   It is, besides, too wide-spread a method for
consulting the future to belong exclusively to any one country
or religious system.   At the same time one should be willing,
after a careful consideration of the facts presented, to admit
that in the Egyptian healing-oracles a system of hypnotism
was known and practiced, and upon the spread of the worship
of Isis and Serapis, in the time of the Ptolemies, that the
similarity in ritual to that of the Greek dream-gods led to
the incorporation of many features of the Egyptian cults into
the Greek ritual.   The temples of Isis and Asklepios were not
far apart in Tithorea[3] and in Kenchreiai,[4] and in Boiai Serapis
and Isis shared a temple with Asklepios,[5] while in the temple
of Apollo in Aigeira their statues were near that of Asklepios.[6]
A priest of Asklepios in a temple in Dacia dedicated a tablet
to Serapis.[7]   The general type of Asklepios and Serapis was
the same, so that Aristides saw them in a vision wonderfully
like each other.[8]   This similarity in divinity and ritual was
not without its effect upon the Greek cult, and one cannot
doubt that the practice of hypnotism was introduced in the later
years of the cult.

The following are the cures which are to be classed under
this head : a man having all his fingers but one paralyzed,
came as a suppliant to the god.   And seeing the records of
the cures, he had no faith in them, but ridiculed what was
written.   Going to sleep, he had a vision ; it seemed that as

[1] Diodor. I. 25.   [2] Strab. XVII. 1, 17.   [3] Paus. X. 32, 13.
[4] Paus. II. 2, 3.   Isis comes into relation with Asklepios in Pagai.   Jour. Hell.
Stud. VIII. 50.
[5] Paus. III. 22, 13.   [6] Paus. VII. 26, 7.
[7] CIL. III. 1, 973.   [8] Aristid. 500, 19.

he was playing at astragals by the temples and was about to make a throw, the god appeared and leaped upon his hand and stretched out his fingers. When the god had stepped off, it seemed that he bent his hand together himself, and stretched out each finger. When they were all straightened out, the god asked him if he still would disbelieve the records in the temple, and he said, " No."

" Then because formerly you were incredulous, you shall have the more occasion to assert, 'I am now incredulous of nothing which is not incredible.' " [1]

A lame man is told to go down a ladder, and his lameness is cured.[2] A paralytic man being told to go and fetch the largest stone he can into the Hieron, brings the stone which lay before the ἄβατον.[3]

Magnetic treatment, rubbing and laying on of hands played some part in the cures. Its value had been known for a long time,[4] and Aristophanes saw it in Athens.[5] A blind man's sight was restored by the fingers of the god,[6] and a barren woman received help in the same way.[7] Besides the evidence of the stéles, there are a few allusions in literature to the healing hand of Asklepios.[8]

The remaining cures recorded in Epidauros, if cures and not fictions to impose upon suppliants, are inexplicable. As they stand, they are miracles, pure and simple, and between them and those of the New Testament there is a striking parallelism, as has been noticed by Baunack, pages 145 and 146. Women came to the temple praying for the delivery of their

---

[1] Bau. 59, 22. For conjectural readings in the last few lines, see Bau. p. 122, note 6, and Merriam in Gaillard's Medical Journal, May, 1885.

[2] Bau. 80, 87.   [3] Bau. 59, 107.

[4] Solon Frag. 13.

πολλάκι δ' ἐξ ὀλίγης ὀδύνης μέγα γίγνεται ἄλγος
κ' οὐκ ἂν τις λύσαιτ' ἤπια φάρμακα δούς
τὸν δὲ κακαῖς νούσοισι κυκώμενον ἀργαλέαις τε
ἁψάμενος χειροῖν αἶψα τίθησ' ὑγιῆ.

[5] Arist. Plut. 728.   [6] Bau. 59, 120.   [7] Bau. 80, 61.

[8] Aelian. ἀποσπ. 99. Julian, Ep. 34, 406 d; 61, 450 a. Suid. art. Θεόπομπος.

children, and in the morning the children were born.[1] A dumb
boy came to the temple with his father. After the sacrifice
was made, the fire-bearer of the god turned to the father and
said, "Will you promise to pay the fees within a year if you
gain your object in coming?" And the boy suddenly cried, "I
promise." And his father in astonishment bade him speak
again, which he did, and was cured.[2] The blind were cured by
the night's sleep in the temple.[3] Pausanias tells a legend of
the temple of Asklepios at Naupaktos about another person
miraculously cured of blindness. The temple was built by one
Phalysios, who had an ailment in his eyes and was nearly blind.
The god of Epidauros sent to him the poetess Anyte with a
sealed letter, which she found in her hands on awaking from
a vision of the god. She sailed to Naupaktos and bade Phalysios remove the seal and read what was written. Though he was
clearly unable to read from his blindness, yet, with faith in the
god, having broken open the seal, he became cured by looking
at the letter, and gave Anyte two thousand gold staters, which
was the sum mentioned in the letter.[4] One of the inscriptions
notes an establishment of another Asklepieion under similar
circumstances.[5] A lame man's crutch was stolen by a boy, but
the lame man rose and gave chase.[6] A man whose knees were
powerless saw a vision in which the attendants bore him before
the temple, and the god, having yoked his horses into a chariot,
drove upon him and forthwith he was cured.[7] A paralytic was
taken by attendants and laid in a pool whose waters made him
strong again.[8] In one case a broken cup was mended.[9] A
father whose child was lost, slept in the ἄβατον and had a vision
in which the god led him to the place where he afterwards found
the child.[10]

The use of dogs and serpents in the temples as a means of
healing is remarkable. A child was cured of a growth on his

---

[1] Bau. 59, 3 ; 80, 83.   [2] Bau. 59, 41.   [3] Bau. 59, 90 ; 80, 7.
[4] Paus. X. 38, 13.   [5] Bau. 80, 81.   [6] Bau. 59, 111.
[7] Bau. 80, 110.   [8] Bau. 80, 102.   [9] Bau. 59, 79.   [10] Bau. 80, 19.

neck by the tongue of a dog.[1] A blind boy received his sight
in the same way.[2] Aristophanes gives evidence of the use of
serpents in Athens.[3] In Epidauros a man suffering from an
ulcer on his toe, was brought to a seat where he fell asleep.
A serpent came and with his tongue healed the toe and then
glided back into the ἄβατον. In the vision it had seemed that
a beautiful youth applied some ointment to his toe.[4] A child-
less woman was aided by a serpent which crawled over her.[5]

If now, from the records of an early period in the history of
the Asklepieia, we turn to accounts of the first and second
centuries after Christ, we find a marked change in the system
of medical procedure. The main sources of information are,
first, the inscription of M. Julius Apellas, in Epidauros, in the
reign of Antoninus Pius ;[6] second, the discourses of Aristides
Rhetor ;[7] third, a few inscriptions from the island of Tiberina ;[8]
fourth, a Cretan inscription of the first century before Christ.[9]

According to these, the cures were effected by courses of
treatment which were suggested to the patients in sleep.
There is no trace of a miracle left. Plenty of exercise, frequent use of baths, hot and cold, a carefully regulated diet,
few medicines, and above all, a cheerful temper and restful
surroundings, these are the later means employed. The physician no longer directly applies his heroic remedies ; either in
hypnotic state the patient prescribes for himself, or his treatment is suggested by the physicians during the night or in

---

[1] Bau. 80, 35.

[2] Bau. 59, 126. M. Gaidoz in Rev. Arch., 1884, II. p. 217 ff., discusses the
"widespread belief in the curative power of the dog's tongue, for sores." Superstition has long held to the belief in the similar power of reptiles. Porphyry
furnishes an illustration. "For we see that those who are blind recover their sight
by eating a viper. A servant of Cratenus, the physician, happening to be seized
with a new kind of disease in which the flesh fell away from the bones, derived
no benefit from the medicines ; but by eating a viper prepared after the manner
of a fish, the flesh became conglutinated to the bones, and he was restored to
health."

[3] Arist. Plut. 732–36.   [4] Bau. 59, 113.   [5] Bau. 80, 117.
[6] Bau. 60.   [7] Aristid. Ἱερῶν λόγοι.   [8] CIG. 5980.
[9] Philol. 1889, p. 401 ; 1890, p. 577 ff.

the morning.   The sanctuary has become a sanitarium.   Here
is a body of skilled men trained by tradition and experience.

To review briefly : — The earliest form of the cult was a worship of Asklepios, and a consultation by dreams, at first for
any purpose, and eventually for health.   At this time there
were no physicians ; then the oracle became more famous for
its success in performing cures and the priest aided in interpretation of dreams by his practical knowledge of simple remedies.
Third, some priest gave all his attention to observance of ritual,
while a colleague or assistant devoted himself to the cures,
which were effected by surgical operations, magnetism, drugs,
or applications of the dogs or serpents.   The last stage was
reached when a school of physicians called Asklepiadæ became
a recognized factor in the temples, and the cult and the oracle
were divorced.   The cures were not the work of a night, but
the result of an extended course of treatment.

CHAPTER VI.

PUBLIC CEREMONIAL.

As the cult of Asklepios assumed greater proportions, it came more into the notice of the state as a whole, and like older and more important cults received the homage of the government. Nor is this unnatural, for the health of the community is a matter of general interest. The introduction of Asklepios into Rome was the result of state legislation on the occasion of a plague in that city. Expressions of public recognition of the cult come to hand more frequently in Athens than elsewhere, either because there the religion was under state control, or the evidence in other towns is lacking through want of material for investigation.

The priest offered certain sacrifices in behalf of the state during the year at intervals which had been fixed by law.[1] In Kos there was a public sacrifice, each month, of a victim, the price of which was a hundred drachmas.[2] Other special sacrifices were occasionally decreed for the health of the "Boulê, the citizens and their wives and children," and were offered both to Asklepios and Hygieia, and to the other gods who had altars in the Asklepieion. The priest observed the omens at the ceremony and reported them publicly. Sometimes the sacrifices were made for the colonists of Athens as well as her citizens.[3] Such offerings took place not alone in the Asklepieion, for the city prayed for health and preservation at many shrines. A decree of thanks was voted at the end of the year to the priest, and set in the temple of Asklepios.[4] The epithet

---

[1] CIA. II. 1, Add. Nov. 477 b. τὰς θυσίας ἁπάσας τέθυκεν κατὰ (τὰ) ψηφίσματα. CIA. II. 1, Add. Nov. 567 b. τάς τε θυσίας ὅσας πρ[οσῆ]κεν αὐτὸν θῦσαι πάσας καλῶς κα[ὶ] φιλοτίμως τέθυκεν.

[2] BCH. V. 221.   [3] CIA. II. 1, Add. Nov. 477 b.

[4] CIA. II. 1, 453; Add. Nov. 373 b; Add. et Corr. 453 b.

Σωτήρ, so frequent on coins, in inscriptions and literature, is commonly given to Asklepios and Hygieia as guardians of a city. The sense of the protecting power of these gods was further expressed by the addition of such epithets as πολιοῦχος or πατρῷος.[1]

The different political or religious organizations voted special dedications to the healing gods. Such decrees remain from the Council of the Areiopagos [2] and the Ephebes of Telesphoros.[3] The Orgeones held a shrine of Asklepios in the deme Prospalta, where they carried on a special ritual.[4] Physicians in Athens were obliged to offer to Asklepios and Hygieia public sacrifices for themselves and their patients.[5]

The sacrifices made either at the consecration of a priest or at the beginning of a new year were called εἰσιτητήρια [6] or better, εἰσιτήρια. These were customary in other cults.[7] An individual used to give public thanks for a cure, and the people as a whole congratulated him on his recovery,[8] or a public sacrifice was offered for the benefit of a citizen.[9]

The kind of sacrifice offered by the state was different from that of individuals. The victim was an ox or bull [10]; the reliefs which show only a cow or ram represent a private offering. For the public sacrifice the temple was magnificently adorned.[11] The images of Asklepios and Hygieia were placed on couches, and tables stood near for the offerings.

An important feature of the public ritual was singing the pæan, a song which was the orthodox version of the birth and

---

[1] IGS. et I. 402.   Cf. Julian. Orat. IV. 153 B.   · · · τὸν σωτῆρα τῶν ὅλων ἀπογεννήσας 'Ασκληπιόν · · ·.   BCH. V. 229.

[2] CIA. III. 1, Add. et Corr. 77 a.   [3] CIA. III. 1, 1159.

[4] CIA. II. 2, 990.   [5] CIA. II. 1, Add. Nov. 352 b; II. 3, 1449.

[6] CIA. II. 1, Add. et Corr. 453 b and c.

[7] Before the sessions of the Boulê the εἰσητήρια were offered by the ἱεροποιοί. Demosth. Mid. 114.

[8] CIG. 5980, ll. 10, 14, 18.   [9] Aristid. 531, 8.

[10] CIA. II. 1, Add. et Corr. 453 b and c.   CIG. 3538.   Polyb. 32, 27, 1.   Paus. II. 11, 7.   Wroth, Asklepios and the Coins of Pergamon, p. 46.

[11] 'Αθήν. VI. 134, n. 9, l. 16.

life of Asklepios. In Epidauros, on the occasion of the yearly
festival, the noblest citizens, with long flowing hair, clad in
white, and bearing laurel wreaths and branches of blossom-
ing olive, marched solemnly out from the city to the valley
where lay the Asklepieion, chanting hymns of praise to Apollo
and Asklepios. At the temple, prayers were offered for the
health of the citizens and their offspring, as well as for the
general peace and welfare of the town, for Asklepios was
preëminently the patron of Epidauros.[1]   In other temples,
boys who assisted the priest by lighting the altar-fires, swing-
ing the incense and performing other light duties, formed the
choir and chanted responsively or in unison the sacred tradition.   One hundred such formed the choir in Ptolemäis, and
probably also in Athens, for so similar are the pæans which
were sung, that the Egyptian ritual must have been closely
related to that in Attica.[2]   As part of the public ritual, singing
took place both in the processions and while the priest was
officiating at the altar.   At a sacrifice in Pergamon to Zeus,
Athena, Dionysos and Asklepios, the offering, a bull, was
divided into four parts, and the chorus of voices sang to each
god in turn as his share was laid before his cult-statue.[3] Here,
too, a series of hymns to the hero Telephos were sung in the
Asklepieion,[4] a hint of a cult of Telephos which was supplanted
by the greater divinity.

Some of the Asklepios pæans have come down to us. In
literature are found frequent allusions to them and their composition.   Those which are best preserved are from Epidauros,
Athens, Ptolemäis and Rome.[5]   That from Epidauros expresses
earnestly and poetically the feeling of dependence and worship
in the hearts of the people.   The Athenian pæans, and the
similar pæan from Egypt, on the other hand, consist of a

---

[1] Bau. 84, 10–26.   [2] Rev. Arch. 1889, p. 71.
[3] CIG. 3538.   [4] Paus. III. 26, 10.
[5] Isyl. v. Epid.   CIA. III. 1, 171;   Add. et Corr. 171 b, c, d, g, k.   Rev. Arch.
1889, p. 71.   CIG. 5973 c.

jumble of epithets hung indiscriminately on the bare branches
of Asklepios's genealogical tree. The Roman songs to Asklepios, Hygieia and Telesphoros are somewhat better, but leave
much to be desired. The pæan of Sophocles has been discussed
elsewhere.[1]

A characteristically Greek form of worship was the establishment of periodical festivals in honor of this or that deity.
Asklepios received his share too, and abundant evidence from
literary sources, inscriptions and coins proves his festivals to
have been not the least important in the Greek calendar. The
earliest literary mention of the festivals at Epidauros is in
the third Nemean Ode in connection with the Nemean and
Megarian games.[2] The Scholiast tells us that games were
held in Epidauros in honor of Asklepios every third year, at
first by the Asklepiadae, and afterwards by the Argives.
This festival came in the second year of each Olympiad,
for it took place before the Panathenaia, and nine days
after the Isthmian games.[3] The latter were held in the
second and fourth of each Olympiad, alternately in summer
and spring. As the Panathenaia was in the summer, the
Epidaurian games came in early autumn. Nissen dates
them exactly on September fifth.[4] Contests were held in
Kos every fifth year with special magnificence in connection
with the Dionysiac festival.[5] These were called τὰ μεγάλα
'Ασκλάπεια, distinguishing them from the annual festivals.[6]
The same expression occurs in Ankyra[7] and Thyateira.[8] A
festival in Kos under the title of τῆς ῥάβδου ἡ ἀνάληψις is
mentioned by Hippocrates once. What the meaning or nature
of this ceremony was, is not known. It is dependent for
explanation upon the significance of the staff which is almost

---

[1] Chap. II. p. 29, and notes.   [2] Pind. Nem. III. 145.
[3] Plato, Ion. I.
[4] Nissen. Ueber Tempel-Orientirung. Rh. Mus. 42, p. 46.
[5] Ditt. 398, 13. 'Ασκληπίεια τὰ ἐν κῷ · · ·. BCH. V. 211, 16. · · · ἐν τῷ θεάτρῳ
Διονυσίοις τοῖς πρώτοις καὶ τοῖς 'Ασκλαπιείοις γινομένοις κατὰ πανήγυριν · · ·.
[6] Ditt. 399, 8.   [7] CIG. 4016 and 4017.   [8] BCH. X. 415, n. 24.

as common an attribute of Asklepios as the serpent. If the
staff is the symbol of the wide wandering of the god, may
not the "taking up the staff" be symbolic of one of his
journeys? If so, in Kos, his journey to that island may be
meant, and the ceremony be a dramatic representation of
the introduction of the cult. It seems to have been merely
a special rite, for Hippocrates says that on the same day
occurred the annual national festival.[1] The phrase κατὰ
πανήγυριν also occurs elsewhere.[2]

At Athens the Asklepieia were of slight importance. The
ceremonies took place on the eighth of the month Elaphebolion,
March-April.[3] An inscription places the Asklepieia between
the Lenaean and the Dionysiac festivals, and shows that they
were under the charge of the public overseer of offerings, and
that the money from the sale of hides at the festivals amounted
to two hundred ninety-one drachmas at one time, and two hundred seventy-one at another.[4] No contests took place as far as
we know. Pæans were sung at early morning,[5] and then came
ἡ θυσία καὶ ὁ προαγών. Mommsen has suggested that the
προαγών was a preparatory representation which took place in
the theatre in honor of Dionysos, a rehearsal of plays to follow
in the Dionysiac festival.[6] At Lampsakos the Asklepieia were
very elaborate. The expenses were shared by the citizens
who kept holiday during the festival and came to the celebration wearing wreaths of laurel and oleander which the priest
supplied. There was a list kept of those who came.[7] In

---

[1] Hippoc. Ep. 13. Ed. Kühn, 778. καὶ ἔτυχε τότ᾽ ἐοῦσα τῆς ῥάβδου ἡ ἀνάληψις ἐν
ἐκείνῃ τῇ ἡμέρᾳ καὶ ἐτήσιος ἑορτή, ὡς ἴστε, πανήγυρις ἡμῖν καὶ πομπὴ πολυτελὴς ἐς
κυπάρισσον ἦν ἔθος ἀνάγειν τοῖς τῷ θεῷ προσήκουσιν · · ·.

[2] Bau. 10.

[3] Aesch. Ctes. p. 455. ἐκκλησίαν ποιεῖν τοὺς πρυτάνεις τῇ ὀγδόῃ ἱσταμένου τοῦ
ἐλαφηβολιῶνος μηνός, ὅτ᾽ ἦν τῷ Ἀσκληπιῷ ἡ θυσία καὶ ὁ προαγών, ἐν τῇ ἱερᾷ ἡμέρᾳ · · ·.
Nissen. Rh. Mus. 40, p. 340.

[4] CIA. II. 2, 741.

[5] Suid. ἀσκωλίαζε · καὶ ὄρθριον ᾀδομένου τοῦ παιᾶνος τῷ Ἀσκληπιῷ.

[6] Heortology, p. 391 ff. Hiller, in Hermes VII. p. 393 ff.

[7] CIG. 3641 b.

Epidauros and Kos the chief interest centered in the games which were held in the groves. They consisted of athletic contests and trials of skill in music and poetry.[1] The direction of the games was in charge of one of the citizens, and the towns in Argos voted special honors to such an one. Decrees of this character come from Epidauros and Hermione.[2] It may have been customary for the victor to make some special dedication to Asklepios as a thank-offering.[3]

While the Asklepieia were insignificant in Athens, there was one public ceremony peculiar to the Athenian cult, which is of considerable importance, as it is an expression of the mystical features which the cult assumed in Athens alone. In the Epidauria Asklepios comes in contact with the mysterious divinities of the lower world, and for one day in the year takes his place by them. The legend of the establishment of the Epidauria during the celebration of the Eleusinia is, that Asklepios himself came from Epidauros on the second day to take part in the mysteries, and that he was initiated upon that day, being too late to join the throng of initiates who assembled on the day before.[4] The Eleusinian mysteries began with assembly and purification on the sixteenth of the month Boedromion. The next day occurred the sacrifices in the city, and on the evening of that day the Epidauria began[5] with a ceremony which lasted

---

[1] The slight information we have of these games comes from Plato in the opening sentences of the Ion, the mention by Hippocrates of the procession to the cypress grove, and inscriptions on coins which testify merely to the existence of the games. We know of the victories of one Nikokles of Athens who played the cithara and gained many prizes, CIA. II. 3, 1367, and racing was another form of contest. CIG. 1515 *a*, 5 and *b*, 4. · · · Ἀσκλήπεια παῖδας δόλιχον. The pentathlon was in use in Kos, Ditt. 399. For the towns from which Asklepieia are reported, see the General Index under the heading *Festivals*.

[2] CIG. 1165; 1186. Bau. 10; 32. Coll. 3290.   [3] CIG. 1171.

[4] Philost. Vit. Apoll. IV. 18, p. 72. ἦν μὲν δὴ Ἐπιδαυρίων ἡμέρα. τὰ δὲ Ἐπιδαύρια μετὰ πρόρρησίν τε καὶ ἱερεῖα δεῦρο μυεῖν Ἀθηναίοις πάτριον ἐπὶ θυσίᾳ δευτέρᾳ, τουτὶ δὲ ἐνόμισαν Ἀσκληπιοῦ ἕνεκα, ὅτι δὴ ἐμύησαν αὐτὸν ἥκοντα Ἐπιδαύροθεν ὀψὲ μυστηρίων. Pausanias recognizes in the name of the special day which was sacred to Asklepios the derivation of the Athenian cult from Epidauros. II. 26, 8.

[5] Girard, p. 41. Mommsen, p. 226.

throughout the night, παννυχίς, in which the devout slept in the Asklepieion.[1] The παννυχίς preceded other festivals, as that of Poseidon,[2] the Panathenaia,[3] and the Heroia in the Asklepieion.[4] Early in the morning the sacrifice took place, and other rites of which we know little. There is every reason to suppose that the initiation rites were repeated with either the cult-statue or a priest as initiate. The κανηφόροι and ἀρρηφόροι[5] took part in the procession of this day, being appointed expressly for this purpose.[6] The sacred ciste, which is represented in reliefs from the Asklepieion,[7] was carried in this procession, for it is found in connection with the mystery processions of Eleusis and of Isis and Osiris at Rome. Its only possible significance in the Asklepios cult must be as an expression of the relation of Asklepios to the mysteries. It contained perhaps objects for sacrifice, but its importance in ritual was due to the fact that holy symbols were carried in it.[8] The Ephebes joined in this ceremony.[9] A relief of the first half of the fourth century represents Asklepios with Demeter and Persephone, which hints at the initiation without giving any clue to its method.[10] The goddesses had an altar in the Asklepieion, and were honored in Epidauros.[11]

There was at Athens a third festival, ἡρῷα, which bears in its name its character — a celebration in honor of the Hero Asklepios. It has been shown that in Athens alone the god had this character in ritual, although legends point to him as a

---

[1] CIA. II. 1, Add. et Corr. 453 b; Add. Nov. 373 b. Mommsen, p. 253.

[2] Aristid. 446, 18.

[3] CIA. II. 1, 163.

[4] CIA. II. 1, Add. et Corr. 453 b.

[5] CIA. II. 1, Add. et Corr. 453 b; III. 1, 916.

[6] CIA. III. 1, 916. ··· κανηφορήσασαν Ἐπιδαυρίοις.
CIA. III. 1, 921. ··· κανηφορήσασαν Ἀσκληπιῷ.

[7] BCH. II. pl. VII.

[8] Otto Jahn. Die Cista Mystika. Hermes III. p. 317 ff.

[9] Köhler. Mitth. d. Arch. Inst. IV. p. 335.

[10] Mitth. d. Arch. Inst. II. pl. XVIII. Girard, pl. II.

[11] Bau. 60, 14. Bau. Aus Epidauros, p. 2. Coll. 3396.

hero. Two inscriptions mention the Heroia,[1] but there is no other known evidence of such a festival. Köhler has rightly called attention to the connection between this and the presence of so many reliefs in the Asklepieion which are plainly funeral-feasts.[2] Girard, on the other hand, rejects any theory which would connect death with a sanctuary which must not be polluted either by birth or death, and leaves a choice of other explanations. His objections do not seem valid, for the ceremony in honor of the Hero Asklepios in a shrine where there was no grave would be so removed from thought of his death as not to disturb the holiness of the shrine.

---

[1] CIA. II. 1, Add. et Corr. 453 *b* and *c*.
[2] Mitth. d. Arch. Inst. II. pp. 245 and 254.

CHAPTER VII.

RITUAL OF THE INDIVIDUAL.

THE fame and popularity of the Asklepios cult were due to its practical side. The same faith which even to this day impels hundreds to seek health at obscure wells said to have miraculous power, was more potent at the time when medical science was in its infancy and diseases were believed to be the work of a malignant demon. And this side of the cult continued long after the god Asklepios ceased to be. It is an accepted fact that many rites of the Christian church are adopted from the religious ceremonies of the people who in adopting the new system changed their faith in name only. There prevails in Greece to this day the practice of sleeping at the feet of the images of the saints.[1] A careful study of the beliefs óf the folk in Catholic countries would reveal a mass of customs directly derived from the ritual of the Greek healing gods. Beside the pictures of the Mother of God hang models of legs, arms, or other parts of the body, just as in temples of old. An array of crutches stands against the wall, and bits of cardboard with words of thanksgiving printed upon them lie about. The contented expression in the face of the sick child which has been taken into the arms of the Holbein Madonna embodies the faith that a touch of the divine hand, $\pi\alpha\iota\acute{\omega}\nu\iota\sigma\varsigma\ \chi\epsilon\acute{\iota}\rho$, is sufficient to restore to health. And who shall say whether these customs are "heathen" or "Christian"? They are neither; they are intensely human, an utterance of the helplessness of persons in affliction crying out for the aid of a power not themselves that works for righteousness.

---

[1] Bernh. Schmidt. Das Volksleben der Neugriechen u. das hellenische Alterthum. Leipzig, 1871.

He who wished to consult Asklepios came at evening, and before engaging in any ceremony saw that his body was clean. "It is necessary, therefore, that, being purified in our own manner, we should make oblations, offering to the gods those sacrifices which are pleasing to them and not such as are attended with great expense. Now, however, if a man's body is not pure and invested with a splendid garment, he does not think it is qualified for the sanctity of sacrifice." In Epidauros, therefore, there was the following inscription on the doors of the temple :

> " Into an odorous temple, he who goes
> Should pure and holy be ; but to be wise
> In what to sanctity pertains, is to be pure." [1]

The suppliant first bathed in cold water, — a rite which was at once hygienic and symbolic. This purification was sometimes preceded by a prayer to the god.[2] The use of salt water for this purpose·was frequent, as is noticed by historians and poets, especially the tragedians. The women of Tanagra who were initiated into the rites of Dionysos went into the sea,[3] and the statue of Artemis, made unclean by the touch of Orestes, was purified by salt water.[4] The victims for the sacrifice to the Eleusinian goddesses were washed in the sea. As soon as the god Plutos entered the Asklepieion he was bathed in the θάλασσα.[5] The Scholiast reminds us that it was the custom for the ancients to bathe in the sea before sacrificing, quoting from Homer.[6] Girard, however, explains the use of this word not as meaning that the god was taken to the harbor at Athens, but that a salt bath was given in the Asklepieion. The spring there was, and still is, of a brackish taste, and the θάλασσα may be intended to convey this idea. Herodotus speaks of the salt spring struck by Poseidon on the north of

---

[1] Porphyry, de Abstin. Anim. II. 17.   Cf. Coll. 3472.
[2] Aristid. 479, 2.   [3] Paus. IX. 20, 4.
[4] Eurip. Iph. Tau. 1034.   [5] Arist. Plut. 656.
[6] A 314. B 261.

the Erechtheion as a θάλασσα,[1] and modern Greek calls all salt water by this name, whether connected with the sea or not.[2]

Each suppliant brought what he needed for the night, a mattress,[3] and cakes for the sacrifice which took place before sleeping.[4] The cakes were thin, flat, and round, made of wheat or barley, and pierced with holes.[5] They were sweetened[6] and dipped in wine, oil, or honey.[7] The cakes and incense were burned on the altar.[8] This was the usual sacrifice of the very poor. Food may also have been brought for the suppliant's own use, for Aristophanes tells of the old woman who had porridge by her during the night.[9] White gowns were the rule in the Asklepieia both for priests and suppliants.[10] It is an old superstition that to sleep in white induced dreams.[11] Suppliants too ill to come to the temple sent prayers for recovery, which were inscribed and set in the sanctuary. An example is found at Epidauros, where the patient had been encouraged previously by a vision of the god.[12] Or some one may dream for the sick person, either a friend or the priest himself.[13]

---

[1] Hdt. VIII. 55.   [2] Girard, p. 70 ff.   [3] Arist. Plut. 663.

[4] Sch. Arist. Plut. 660. προθύματα · τὰ πρὸ τῆς θυσίας γενόμενα θυμιάματα. Bau. 59, 42. ὡς δὲ προεθύσατο καὶ ἐπόησε τὰ νομιζόμενα. Bau. 59, 93. καθικετεύσας τὸν θεὸν ἐνεκάθευδε. Cf. Bau. 80, 101. A single passage in Aristides shows that the suppliant knelt during some part of the service. καὶ ἔδει τὸ γόνυ τὸ δεξιὸν κλίναντα ἱκετεύειν τε καὶ καλεῖν Λύσιον τὸν θεόν.

[5] Suid. πλακούντια πλατέα καὶ λεπτὰ καὶ περιφερῆ. Hesych. πλακούντια ἀπὸ ἄρτου.

[6] Sch. Arist. Plut. 660. γλυκύσματα.

[7] Sch. Arist. Pax, 1040.

[8] Arist. Plut. 660. ἐπεὶ δὲ βωμῷ πόπανα καὶ θυλήματα καθωσιώθη μέλανος Ἡφαίστου φλογί. Hesych. θυλήματα · βεβρεγμένα μέλιτι ἄλφιτα, ἢ θυμιάματα ἐπὶ βωμῶν. Cf. Aristid. 517, 14 ; 64, 2. Philost. Vit. Soph. p. 266. Bau. 60, 19.

[9] Arist. Plut. 683.

[10] Aristid. 473, 8. ἐν τῷ θεάτρῳ τῷ ἱερῷ πλῆθος ἀνθρώπων εἶναι λευχειμονούντων καὶ συνεληλυθότων κατὰ τὸν θεόν. Aristid. 494, 6. λευχείμων καὶ ἐζωσμένος. Cf. Le Bas II. 326 a, l. 16, and Pæan of Isyllos.

[11] Θ 278. Ψ 198.   [12] Bau. Aus Epid. p. 13.

[13] Bau. 80, 1. Herodotus writes that Mus after consulting various oracles for Mardonius, κατεκοίμησε ἐς Ἀμφιάρεω. VIII. 134. Again in Strab. XVII. 1, 17. ἐγκοιμᾶσθαι αὐτοὺς ὑπὲρ ἑαυτῶν ἢ ἑτέρους. In the temple of Pluto near Nysa the priests directed cures by their own visions. Strab. XIV. 1, 44. λέγουσι γὰρ δὴ καὶ

When an .individual or a family sacrificed animals, the small
domestic animals were used, such as swine, rams, goats, and
cocks.[1] The information about the sacrifice of goats is very
definite. In general, they are not to be offered.[2] In Epidauros
their sacrifice was expressly forbidden, while in Kyrene, whose
cult was derived from Epidauros, there was no such restriction.[3]
At Tithorea every sort. of animal could be sacrificed to Asklepios but goats.[4] At Athens goats were offered.[5] A meaningless explanation of the sacrifice of goats is offered by Servius
in a comment on Virgil's Georgics, II. 380. "*Item capra im-
molatur Aesculapio, qui est deus salutis, cum capra nunquam
sine febre sit.*" In the Peloponnesian myth the goat appears
as the nurse of the child Asklepios, and as such is found on
coins and in Aigeira with an image of the child.[6] If the myth
is given as the reason for the sacredness of the animal, the
cause and effect have changed places. First the goat was
sacred to Asklepios, and then rose the ætiological myth.

From the closing scene of the Phaedo we are familiar with
the sacrifice of a "cock to Asklepios."[7] Brunn believes that
one is represented in an Asklepios relief in the Glyptothek
in München,[8] and it is found on coins of fifth century before
Christ. From Selinus in Sicily we find the cock before the
altar of Asklepios.[9] The cock is not peculiar as a sacrifice

τοὺς νοσώδεις καὶ προσέχοντας ταῖς τῶν θεῶν τούτων θεραπείαις φοιτᾶν ἐκεῖσε καὶ διαι-
τᾶσθαι ἐν τῇ κώμῃ πλησίον τοῦ Ἄντρου παρὰ τοῖς ἐμπείροις τῶν ἱερέων, οἱ ἐγκοιμῶνταί τε
ὑπὲρ αὐτῶν καὶ διατάττουσιν ἐκ τῶν ὀνείρων τὰς θεραπείας. Aristides had dreams
which coincided with those of the neocore. 473, 6.

[1] Le Bas, Voy. Arch. pl. 104. Mitth. d. Arch. Inst.̇IV. p. 126, 2. AZ. 1877,
p. 147, 15. BCH. II. p. 70. See the General Index under the heading *Animal
Sacrifice.* A coin from Aigai in Kilikia bears Asklepios, Telesphoros and a kid,
evidently an offering. Mionn. S VII. 157, 34. A similar coin from Pergamon
has a small animal which Mr. Wroth identifies as a rat gnawing, and so not an
offering. This is an attribute of Apollo Σμινθεύς, and its presence on the Asklepios coin points to an association of the two cults at Pergamon. W. Wroth,
Asklepios and the Coins of Pergamon.

[2] Sext. Emp. Pyrrh. hypot. 3, 220. [3] Paus. II. 26, 9.
[4] Paus. X. 32, 12. [5] BCH. II. pl. VII.
[6] AZ. 1862, 282*. [7] Plato, Phaedo, 118 A. Artemid. Oneir. V. 9.
[8] Brunn, Catalog, n. 85 *a.* [9] Head, Hist. Num. p. 147.

to Asklepios, but is offered to Hermes, Ares, Helios, Kore, and to heroes particularly. It may be that Asklepios is thought of in the last category when the cock is offered. A cock was undoubtedly considered peculiarly sacred to the god, although the attempts by the ancients to explain it only result in a confusion of statements which only show that in some way it was used in the cult, either as means of cure or in the performance of ritual.[1] Yet the best reason for the sacrifice may be the simplest — the ease with which fowls are procured on account of their size and price. In the fourth Mime of Herondas, two women consult the oracle of Asklepios and offer a cock, apologizing for the insignificance of the gift.

Illustrations of individual sacrifice are best found in the Athenian reliefs, which show the cult statues of the god with Hygieia standing by, and somewhat smaller figures of a train of suppliants, bringing gifts, both the animal for sacrifice, and fruits. The table by the god receives the offerings.[2] In Titane the animals were not cut up, and all were burned on the ground except birds, which were burned on the altar.[3] The offering was also to be entirely consumed within the enclosure in Epidauros and Titane.[4] In general, a part of the sacrifice went to the priest, and a part the worshiper used himself or divided among the disciples.[5] In the scene from Herondas the drumsticks of the fowl were left for the priest. A citizen of Athens set up a stone near the city marking the place sacred to Asklepios and Hygieia, and prescribed the manner of sacrifice for the farmers in the neighborhood. Part of the offering was to go to the founder, εἰσάμενος, and part to the priest, θεηκολῶν, and none to be carried away.[6] The pæan was sung at other times than during a public ceremony. Its use after a recovery was common.[7] In the later period of the cult, when the Asklepieia became resorts in which the patients remained

---

[1] Aelian. ἀποσπ. 98. Suid. art. Ἀλεκτρύονα.
[2] BCH. II. pl. VII. For the fruit offering, see the same volume, p. 73.
[3] Paus. II. 11, 7.   [4] Paus. II. 27, 1.   [5] Aristid. 472, 17.
[6] Ditt. 378. τῶν δὲ κρεῶν μὴ φέρεσθαι.   [7] Sch. Arist. Plut. 636.

until cured, sacrifices were made at intervals during the cure according to the will of the god revealed in dreams. Such was the evidence of Apellas [1] and Aristides.[2] The thank-offerings, ἴατρα, σῶστρα,[3] were of more importance than the propitiatory sacrifices. The offerings take the form of a sacrifice, ἀποθύειν τὰ ἴατρα,[4] or a payment, ἀποδιδόναι τὰ ἴατρα.[5] The priests reserved the privilege of revoking a cure, if the pay were not forthcoming.[6] When not convenient to offer immediately, the payment could be made at some later time,[7] generally within a year.[8] Pausanias tells us that twenty thousand staters of gold were paid for cure of a blind man.[9] Silver was paid in one case.[10] Money was paid for attendance as well as cure, and Apellas had to pay an attic obol to the bath-attendant, although he bathed without assistance.[11] The pay was not always in money. A broken cup, which was mended, was itself dedicated;[12] an image was set up.[13] An incredulous dame left a silver pig as a "memorial of her stupidity."[14] A small boy offered his ten jackstones.[15] It is readily seen that the votive offerings were of a most varied character. The temple inventories are lists of all sorts of appropriate or inappropriate objects. The most common were models of the parts of the body. Reliefs representing the god with his attendants and worshipers have been found in great numbers in Athens. Altars were frequently built and dedicated. Alexander left his breastplate and spear in one Asklepieion,[16] and the old cult statue of Hygieia in Titane, if, indeed, it were Hygieia, was completely covered with locks of hair and rich clothing, offerings of the country women.[17] One suppliant composed a pæan ;

---

[1] Bau. 60.
[2] Aristid. 474, 29. αὐτὸς ἦν ὁ σώζων καὶ ἡμέραν ἐφ' ἡμέρᾳ δωρούμενος.
[3] ἴατρα · μισθοὶ θεραπείας. Hesych. σῶστρα · χαριστήριον.
[4] Bau. 59, 45.
[5] Bau. 60, 20.
[6] Bau. 80, 8.
[7] Bau. 80, 35; 59, 56.
[8] Bau. 59, 45.
[9] Paus. X. 38, 13.
[10] Bau. 87, 8.
[11] Bau. 60, 13.
[12] Bau. 59, 89.
[13] Bau. 59, 61.
[14] Bau. 59, 39.
[15] Bau. 59, 68.
[16] Paus. VIII. 28, 1.
[17] Paus. II. 11, 6.

another marked a stone with the name of the god.   A physician
left an image of a child which was cured by the assistance of
the god.[1]   In Sikyon lay the bones of a whale, which had been
offered by some one threatened with shipwreck,[2] for Asklepios
saved life from accident as well as from disease.[3]

A considerable profit was made by the fines which were paid
into the treasury of the god.   For the most part, the fines
were punishments for unjustly holding a person in slavery.   It
was frequent that the slaves were freed by being dedicated to
the service of the god by their masters,[4] and in Rome the slaves
who were cured at the temple of Asklepios became free.[5]

---

[1] CIG. 5974.   [2] Paus. II. 10, 2.

[3] BCH. II. pp. 86 and 87.   CIA. III. 1, Add. et Corr. 132 *b*.   Aristid. 64, 21.
ὁ τὸ πᾶν ἄγων καὶ νέμων σωτὴρ τῶν ὅλων καὶ φύλαξ τῶν ἀθανάτων.   Cf. CIA. II. 1, 470.

[4] See General Index.   [5] Sueton. V. 25.

EPITHETS OF ASKLEPIOS.

This list does not include those epithets in the Supplement to
Roscher, Lexicon der Mythologie.

ἀγλαόπης (Lakonia). Hesych.

ἀγλαός (Kos). Coin ; Mionn. S VI. 572, 70.

αἰγλαήρ (Lakonia). Hesych.

ἀγλαότιμος acc. Orph. Hymn. 67, 6.

Ἀγνίτας Paus. III. 14, 7.

ἄναξ Bau. Aus. Epid. p. 6.

ἀντίπαλος, νόσων ἀντ. acc. Aelian. H. A. X. 49.

ἀρχαγέτης (Phokis). Paus. X. 32, 12.

Αὐλάνιος Paus. IV. 36, 7. (In Kyparissai from Aulon, a valley.)

βασιλεύς voc. Aelian. H. A. IX. 33. Frequent in Aristides.

Γορτύνιος (Titane). Paus. II. 11, 8.

δαίμων acc. δαι. κλεινότατον. Rev. Arch. 1889, p. 71, 4. voc. δαι. σεμνότατε, ibid. l. 11.

δεσπότης voc. Aristid. 63, 2 ; 65, 22 ; 471, 15; 517, 24 ; 518, 2; 522, 17. Suid. art. Δομνῖνος.

εἰητήρ see Ἐπήκοος.

Ἐπήκοος Bau. Aus Epid. p. 5. Ἐπ. εἰητῆρι. Bau. 54.

Ἐπιδαύριος Clem. Alex. protr. IV. 53. Arnob. III. 21. Cic. de Nat. Deor. III. 34, 83.

Εὔκολος (Epidauros). Bau. 44. Often applied to Chthonian gods and heroes.

Ἐπίκουρος (Alba Julia). CIG. 6815.

Ζεύς Aristid. 64, 18; 464, 18; 456, 16; 516, 13. Galen. (ed. Kühn) IV. p. 28. Bau. 65. CIG. 1198.

ἡγεμών Aristid. 532, 1.

ἰατρός (Kyrene). Paus. II. 26, 9.

ἰητήρ Luc. Θεῶν Ἐκκλ. 6; Θεῶν Διαλ. 26, 2. Suid. art. Ἰάκωβος. Bau. 54; 84, 18. CIG. 3159; 3538.

Καούσιος (Kaus). Paus. VIII. 25, 1.

καταφυγή Aristid. 449, 15.

κλεινότατος see δαίμων. voc. Rev. Arch. 1889, p. 71, 4.

κλυτόμητις Bau. 24.

κοίρανος voc. CIA. II. 3, 1509.

Κοτυλεύς (Therapne). Paus. III. 19, 7. Said to be so called from a wound of Herakles upon the hip, κοτύλη.

κύριος Aristid. 504, 27. (Alba Julia.) CIG. 6815.

Λεοντοῦχος (Ascalon) acc. Marin. Procl. 19.

Λιγεώτης dat. Bau. 62. Named from some locality.

Λυσάνιος (Delos). Mon. gr. 1878, n. 7. p. 45.

μάκαρ see Παιάν.

μέγας Aristid. 467, 2 ; 471, 1. Liban. de Vit. Sua. II. 48B.

μειλίχιον acc. Hippoc. Ep. 17 (ed. Kühn, p. 788) μ. καὶ πρᾶον.

μοιρόνομος Aristid. 473, 22.

ὄρθιος gen. Bau. 28.

Παιάν Bau. Aus Epid. p. 13 Rev. Arch. 1889, p. 71. μάκαρ II. CIG. 3773C.

πατρῷοι dat. (of A. and Hygieia). BCH. V. p. 229; 470; 471.

παῖς Paus. VIII. 25, 11 ; 32, 5.

πάνθειος Bau. 57, 4; 68.

πάτριος Galen. (ed. Kühn) VI. 41.

Περγαμηνός Bau. Aus Epid. p. 14. CIG. 6753. CIL. III. 1, 1417a.

πρᾶος see μειλίχιον:

πολιοῦχοι dat. (of A. and Hygieia). IGS. et I. 402.

Σχοινάτας (Helos). CIG. 1444. see Hesych. σχινάτας, and Wide, Lakon Kult. p. 191.

σωτήρ Aristid. frequently. Aelian. H. A. X. 49. Julian. Orat. IV. 153B. Bau. 42; 57; 58; 61; 62; 76; 85; 97. BCH. I. p. 134 n. 42; IV. p. 378; VII. p. 132, 8, 9, 10; X. 415, n. 23; XI. p. 463, 28. CIA. II. 3, 1461; III. 1, Add. et Corr. 132h and m; 411a; 712a. CIG. 1222; 2056f; 3159; 5976; 5978; 5979; 6753. Coll. 255; 260. Ditt. IGGS. 2808; IGS. et I. 968; 1125.

Τρικκαῖος (Gerenia). Strab. VIII. 4, 4.

Ὕπατος (Paros). Ἀθήν. V. p. 31, n. 22.

Ὑπάτιος (Paros). Ἀθήν. V. p. 34, n. 34.

Ὑπερτελεάτης (Asopos). Paus. III. 22, 9. See Wide, loc. cit.

Ὑπήκοος (Gytheion). Reinach, Chroniques d'Orient, p. 395.

φιλάνθρωπος CIG. 6813.

φιλανθρωπότατος Aelian. H. A. IX. 33; 8, 12. Aristid. 411, 19.

φιλόλαος (Asopos). Paus. III. 22, 9.

φύλαξ Aristid. 64, 22.

χάρμα Rev. Arch. 1889, p. 71, 2. μέγα χ. βροτοισιν.

Augustus, often in Latin inscriptions.

Custos, Stat. Silv. III. 4, 100. c. hominum.

Deus (Spain). CIL. II. 21; 3726; diis magnis et bonis. CIL. III. 1, 1560.

Dominus CIL. VIII. 1, 1267.

INDEX TO LITERATURE AND INSCRIPTIONS.

—◦—

Parentage. FATHER.

Apollo.

Apollod. III. 10, 3, 5. Ap. Rhod.
Arg. IV. 616. Aristid. 65, 2 ; 72,
12. Aristid. Mil. Frag. XXII. in
Sch. Pind. Pyth. III. 14. Asklep.
in Sch. Pind. Pyth. III. 14. Cornut.
(ed. Lang) p. 70, 33. Crinagoras,
XVI. in Anth. Gr. (ed. Jacobs).
Cyrill. c. Jul. VI. 200. Diodor.
IV. 71; V. 74. Eratos. καταστ. VI.
Eudocia Aug. XI. Eurip. Alk. 3.
Euseb. Praep. Ev. III. 13, 16.
Eustath. ad B 732. Galen (ed.
Kühn) XIV. 674. Herond. IV. 3.
Hes. Frag. CI.; XCIX. and CXLI.
in Sch. Pind. Pyth. III. 14; CXLII.
in Sch. Pind. Pyth. III. 48. Hom.
Hymn. XVI. Ister, Frag. XXXVI.
in Hygin. Astr. II. 40. Julian.
Orat. IV. 144 B ; 153 B. Liban.
(ed. Morellus) Decl. XL. 844
D; Exemp. Prog. Vol. I. 52 A.
Luc. Ζεὺς Τρ. 26; πῶς δεῖ, 16; Ἀλεξ.
ἢ ψευδ. 10 ; *ibid.* 14. Olympiodor.
Vit. Plat. (ed. Westermann), p. 4.
Cf. p. 9. Orph. Hymn, 67, 6.
Paus. II. 26, 4 and 7 ; VII. 23, 8.
Pherekyd. Frag. VIII. in Sch.
Pind. Pyth. III. 59. Philost. Vit.
Apoll. III. 44, p. 62. Pind. Pyth.
III. 14. Plato, Rep. III. 408 B.
Porphyry in Euseb. Praep. Ev. II.
2, 34; III. 14, 6. Theocrit. Ep.
VII. 1. CIA. III. 1, 171; Add. et

Corr. 171 *a, b.* CIG. 3538. IGS.
et I. 967. Bau. 84, 18, 46; Rev.
Arch. 1889, p. 71, l. 8. Kaibel,
797. Arnob. VI. 21. Cic. de Nat.
Deor. III. 22, 57; III. 34, 83.
Hygin. Fab. 14; 49; 161; 173;
202; 224; 251; 274; Astr. II. 40.
Io. Laur. Lyd. de Mens. IV. 90.
Lactant. de Fals. Rel. I. 10; de
Or. Err. 4. Macrob. Sat. I. 20, 4.
Minuc. Fel. 22, 5. Ovid, Fasti. I.
290; Met. II. 595 ff.; XV. 639.
Stat. Silv. I. 4. 61; III. 4, 6; III.
4, 69 ff. Tertul. Ad Nat. II. 14.

Aristetes.

Ampel. IX. 8.

Arsippos.

Cic. de Nat. Deor. III. 22, 57. Io.
Laur. Lyd. *loc. cit.*

Hephaistos.

Ampel. IX. 8. Stobaeus, φυσικά, I.
41, 69.

Ischys.

Cic. *loc. cit.* Io. Laur. Lyd. *loc. cit.*

" Lai filius " (Elatos ?)

Ampel. IV. 8.

Lapithas.

Eustath. ad B 732.

Sydykos. Euseb. Praep. Ev. I. 10, 25.

MOTHER.

Aigle.

Bau. 84, 44 ff.

Alkippe.

Ampel. IX. 8.

Arsinoe.

Apollod. III. 10, 3, 5. Aristid. Mil. Frag. XXII. in Sch. Pind. Pyth. III. 14. Asklep. in Sch. Pind. Pyth. III. 14. Hes. Frag. XCIX. and CXLI. in Sch. Pind. Pyth. III. 14. Paus. II. 26, 7; III. 26, 4; IV. 3, 2; IV. 31, 12. Soc. Arg. in Sch. Pind. Pyth. III. 14. Cic. *loc. cit.* Io. Laur. Lyd. *loc. cit.*

Koronis.

Dau. of Phlegyas. Apollod. III. 10, 3, 6. Hes. Frag. CXLII. in Sch. Pind. Pyth. III. 14 and 48. Hom. Hymn. XVI. Paus. II. 26, 3 and 7. Pind. Pyth. III. 14. Bau. 84, 37 ff. IGS. et I. 967. Rev. Arch. 1889, p. 71, l. 10. Hygin. Fab. 161; 202. Ister in Hygin. Astr. II. 40.

In Dotion. Apollod. III. 10, 3, 6. Ap. Rhod. Arg. IV. 616. Hes. Frag. CXLI. in Strab. IX. 5, 22; XIV. 1, 40. Hom. Hymn. XVI. Pherekyd. Frag. VIII. in Sch. Pind. Pyth. III. 59. Pind. Pyth. III. 60.

In Epidauros. Paus. II. 26, 7. Bau. 84, 37 ff.

In Trikka. Eustath. ad B 732. Porphyry in Euseb. Praep. Ev. III. 14, 6. Hygin. Fab. 14.

Not Localized. Aristid. 463, 21. Diodor. IV. 71; V. 74. Eudocia Aug. XI. Euseb. Praep. Ev. II. 2, 34. Herond. IV. 3. Luc. 'Αλεξ. ἡ ψευδ. 14. Paus. IV. 3, 2. CIA. III. 1, 171; Add. et Corr. 171 *b.* CIG. 3538. Arnob. I. 36; VII. 44. Cic. *loc. cit.* Cyrill. c. Jul. VI. 200; Hygin. Fab. 224; 251. Io. Laur. Lyd. *loc. cit.* Ovid, Fasti. I. 290; Met. II. 599; XV. 624.

Name of Aigle. Bau. 84, 45.

Name of Arsinoe. Aristid. Mil. Frag. XXII. in Sch. Pind. Pyth. III. 14.

One of the Titanides. Euseb. Praep. Ev. I. 10, 25.

UNCERTAIN PARENTAGE.

Tarquit. in Lactant. de Fals. Rel. I. 10. Soc. Arg. in Tertul. Ad. Nat. II. 14.

Ischys Legend.

Ischys from Arkadia. Pind. Pyth. III. 45.

Son of Elatos. Hes. Fr. CXLII. in Sch. Pind. Pyth. 14 and 48. Hom. Hymn. ad Ap. 210. Ister, Frag. XXXVI. in Hygin. Astr. II. 40. Paus. II. 26, 6. Pind. Pyth. III. 55. Hygin. Fab. 202. Io. Laur. Lyd. *loc. cit.*

Rival of Apollo. Acusil. Frag. XXV. in Sch. Pind. Pyth. III. 25. Apollod. III. 10, 3, 6. Hom. Hymn. ad Ap. 208–13. Pind. Pyth. III. 25. Ovid, Met. II. 599.

Slain by Apollo. Pherekyd. Frag. VIII. in Sch. Pind. Pyth. III. 59.

Slain by Zeus. Hygin. Fab. 202.

Crow Legend.

Apollod. III. 10, 3, 7. Hes. Frag. CXLII. in Sch. Pind. Pyth. III. 14 and 48. Pherekyd. Frag. VIII. in Sch. Pind. Pyth. III. 59. Hygin. Fab. 202. Ovid, Met. II. 596 ff.

Crow becomes black. Apollod. III. 10, 3, 7. Artemon Perg. Frag. VII. in Sch. Pind. Pyth. III. 48. Hygin. Fab. 202. Ovid, Met. II, 632.

Birth Legend.

Koronis slain.

By Apollo. Apollod. III. 10, 3, 7. Hygin. Fab. 202. Ovid, Met. II. 605. Tertul. Ad Nat. II. 14.

By Artemis. Artemon Perg. Frag. VII. in Sch. Pind. Pyth. III. 48.

Paus. II. 26, 6. Pherekyd. Frag.
VIII. in Sch. Pind.. Pyth. III. 59.
Pind. Pyth. III. 61.

Asklepios rescued.
By Apollo. Apollod. III, 10, 3, 7.
Pind. Pyth. III. 75. Hygin. Fab.
202. Ovid, Met. II. 629.
By Hermes. Paus. II. 26, 6.
*Exposed in Epid., found by Ares-
thanas, guarded by dog, nursed by
goat.* Paus. II. 26, 4.
*Exposed in Thelpusa, found by Au-
tolaos, fed by dove.* Paus. VIII, 25,
11.
Exposed, and nursed by dog. Tarquit. in Lactant. de Fals. Rel. I.
10. Tertul. Ad. Nat. II. 14.

Life of Asklepios.

Educated by Chiron. Ampel. II. 9.
Anonym. Vit. Soph. 8, p. 128.
Apollod. III. 10, 3, 7. Cornut.
p. 70, 33. Dion. Rhod. Frag. VI.
in Sch. Pind. Pyth. I. 109. Eratos.
καταστ. XL. Eudocia Aug. XI.
Eustath. ad Δ 202. Hom. Δ 219.
Just. Mart. Apol. 42. Pherekyd.
Frag. VIII. in Sch. Pind. Pyth. III.
59. Philost. 'Ηρωκ. p. 308. Pind.
Nem. III. 92; Pyth. III. 10 and 80.
Plut. Quaes. Conv. VIII. 1, 2. Soc.
Arg. in Sch. Pind. Nem. III. 92.
Tarquit. in Lactant. de Fals. Rel.
I. 10. Xen. Ven. I. 6. Hygin.
Astr. II. 38. Ovid, Met. II. 630.
In Argonaut. Clem. Alex. Strom. I.
21, 105. Hygin. Fab. 14.
In Calydonian hunt. Hygin. Fab. 173.
Bribery. Athenag. τρεσβ. Ch. 29.
Clem. Alex. protr. II. 30. Cyrill.
c. Jul. VI. 200. Euseb. Praep. Ev.
III. 13, 19. Liban. Decl. XXXIX.
835 A ; XL. 844 D. Pind. Pyth.
III. 96 and Sch. Plato, Rep. III.
408 B. Arnob. IV. 24. Tertul.
Apol. XIV.; Ad. Nat. II. 14.

Raises the dead. Apollod. III. 10,
3, 9. Cornut. p. 70, 33. Cyrill. c.
Jul. VI. 200. Diodor. IV. 71.
Eurip. Alk. 123. Hippol. Omn.
Hoer. Ref. IV. 32. Just. Mart.
Apol. 76; Dial. 167. Liban. Orat.
XIII. 408 B. Paus. II. 26, 5.
Pherekyd. Frag. LXXVI. in Sch.
Eurip. Alk. 1. Pind. Pyth. III.
96. Plato, Rep. III. 408 C. Xen.
Ven. I. 6. Ausonius, Edyl. 335, 3.
Tertul. Ad Nat. II. 14.
In Delphi. Pherekyd. Frag. VIII. in
Sch. Pind. Pyth. III. 96 and Sch.
Eurip. Alk. 1. Hygin. Fab. 251.
Glaukos. Ameles. Chal. Frag. II. in
Apollod. III. 10, 3, 10 and Sch.
Eurip. Alk. 1. Sch. Pind. Pyth.
III. 96. Hygin. Fab. 49; Astr.
II. 14.
Hippolytos. Apollod. III. 10, 3, 10.
Eratos. in Hygin. Astr. II. 14.
Sch. Eurip. Alk. 1. Paus. II.
27, 4. Sch. Pind. Pyth. III. 96.
Staphyl. in Sext. Emp. adv. Math.
I. 261. Hygin. Fab. 49. Lactant.
de Fals. Rel. I. 10.
Hymenaios. Orphica, Frag. 256 (ed.
Abel) in Apollod. III. 10, 3, 10,
Sch. Eurip. Alk. 1 and Sch. Pind.
Pyth. III. 96.
Kapaneus and Lykourgos. Stesichor.
ibid.
Orion. Sch. Pind. Pyth. III. 96.
Telesarch. Frag. I. in Sch. Eurip.
Alk. 1 and Sext. Emp. *loc. cit.*
Tyndareos. Luc. περὶ ὁρχ. 45. Pany-
asis in Apollod. III. 10, 3, 10, Sch.
Eurip. Alk. 1, and Sext. Emp. adv.
Math. I. 261. Sch. Pind. Pyth.
III. 96. Pliny, N. II. 29, 3.
Thebans. Stesichor. in Sext. Emp.
loc. cit.
Power from Gorgon's blood. Apol-
lod. III. 10, 3, 9. Tatian, ad Gr.
XII.

Death by Thunderbolt.

Apollod. III. 10, 4, 1. Clem. Alex.
protr. II. 30. Cyrill. c. Jul. VI.
200. Diodor. IV. 71. Eurip.
Alk. 3; 123. Euseb. Praep. Ev.
II. 2, 34; III. 13, 19; Vit.
Const. III. 56. Hes. Frag. CI. in
Athenag. πρεσβ. ch. 29. Hippol.
Omn. Hoer. Ref. IV. 32. Hippoc.
Ep. 24 (ed. Kühn, p. 810). Just.
Mart. Apol. 56. Luc. θεῶν διάλ.
13, 1; περὶ τῆς Περ. 4 and 24.
Origen, κατὰ Κελσ. III. 22 ff. Hes.,
Pind., Pherekyd., Panyasis, An-
dron, Acusil., and. Eurip. in Philo-
dem περὶ Εὐσεβ. (ed. Gomperz, p. 17).
Philost. Ήρωκ. 308. Pind. Pyth.
III. 100. Plato, Rep. III. 408 c.
Soc. Arg. in Sch. Pind. Pyth. III.
102. Panyasis, Phylarch. (Frag.
XVII.), Polyanth., Staphyl. (Frag.
VIII.), Stesichor., Telesarch. (Frag.
I.), in Sext. Emp. adv. Math. I. 260.
Theophil. Ant. ad Ant. I. 343.
Arnob. I. 41; IV. 24. Cic. de Nat.
Deor. III. 22, 57. Hygin. Fab. 49.
Lactant. de Fals. Rel. I. 10. Minuc.
Fel. 22, 7. Pliny, N. H. 29, 3. Stat.
Silv. I. 4, 65. Tertul. Apol. XIV.
Ad Nat. II. 14.
At Delphi. Pherekyd. Frag. LXXVI.
in Sch. Eurip. Alk. 1.
τέθνηκεν ὑμῶν ὁ Ἀσκ. Tatian. ad Gr. 36.
On account of cures. Polyanth. in
Sext. Emp. adv. Math. I. 262.
Phylarch. Frag. XVII. in Sch.
Alk. 1, Sch. Pind. Pyth. III.
96, and Sext. Emp. adv. Math.
I. 261. Just. Mart. Apol. 56.
Complaint of Hades. Diodor. IV.
71.

Burial.

Arkadia. Cic. *loc. cit.* Io. Laur. Lyd.
loc. cit.
Epidauros. Clement. Recog. X. 24.

Kynosura. Clem. Alex. protr. II. 30.
Cic. *loc. cit.* Io. Laur. Lyd. *loc. cit.*

Constellation.

Eratos. καταστ. (ed. Robert) p. 68.
Hygin. Astr. II. 14. Io. Laur.
Lyd. *loc. cit.*

Becomes a God.

Athenag. Πρεσβ. ch. 29. Hippol.
Omn. Hoer. Ref. IV. 32. Just.
Mart. Apol. 56. Luc. Ζεὺς Τρ.
21. Origen, κατὰ Κελσ. III. 22.
Porphyry, Ep. ad Marc. VII.
Arnob. II. 74. Hygin. Fab. 224.
Q. Fabius Pictor Frag. XVI.

Phoenician Legend.

Damasc. Βίος Ἰσ. in Phot. Bibl.
Vol. II. 352. Philo Bybl. Frag. XX.

Three Aesculapii.

Ampel. IX. 8. Arnob. IV. 15. Cic.
loc. cit. Io. Laur. Lyd. *loc. cit.*

Family Relations. WIFE.

Aglaïa.
Quint. Smyrn. p. h. 6, 492.
Arsinoe.
Sch. Δ 195.
Epione.
Aristid. 79, 5. Aristid. Mil. Frag.
XXII. in Sch. Pind. Pyth. III.
14. Cornut. p. 70, 33. Eudocia
Aug. XI. Paus. II. 29, 1. Hippoc.
Ep. 12 (ed. Kühn, p. 778). Sch. Δ
195. Suid. *art.* Ἠπιόνη. Tzetz.
prooem. in Il. 618. CIA. III. 1,
Add. et Corr. 171 b. Rev. Arch.
1889, p. 71.
Hipponee.
Tzetz. prooem. in Il. 617.
Hygieia.
Orph. Hymn. 67, 7.

674 and 676. Hippoc. Ep. 10;
27 (ed. Kühn, pp. 77 and 818).
Hom. Hymn. XVI. Jambl. de
Pyth. Vit. 208. Julian. Orat. IV.
153 B; Ep. 40, 419 B. Just. Mart.
Apol. 76; Dial. 167. Luc. Δὶς κατ.
1; θεῶν διάλ. 26, 2; θεῶν ἐκκλ. 16;
'Ικαρ. 24; Φιλοψ. 10. Lykophron,
1056. Olympiodor. Vit. Plat. (ed.
Westermann), p. 4. Cf. p. 9.
Orph. Hymn. 67. Paus. II. 26, 5.
Philost. Vit. Apoll. III. 44, p. 62;
Ep. 349. Pind. Pyth. III. 12 and
85. Sch. Pind. Pyth. III. 9. Plato,
Rep. III. 406 C; 407 C; 407 E;
X. 599 C; Sym. 186 E. Plut.
Quaest. Conv. IX. 14, 4; de Curios.
VII. Stobaeus, φυσικά I. 41, 69.
Suid. art. γράμματα. Theocrit. Ep.
VII. 1. Theophylact. II. 6, 12.
Kaibel, 473; 506 a and b; 884.
Arnob. I. 38, 41 and 49; II. 65;
III. 23; VII. 22 and 44. Augustin.
de Civ. Dei III. 12, 8; IV. 22, 5.
Cic. de Nat. Deor. III. 22, 57; Ep.
ad Fam. XIV. 7, 1. Hygin. Astr.
II. 14; Fab. 274. Io. Laur. Lyd.
de Mens. IV. 32. Ovid, Met. XV.
744. Plaut. Men. V. 3, 5. Pliny,
N. H. 7, 160; 25, 13; 30, 69. Tacit.
Hist. IV. 84. Terence, Hec. 338.

Cures. Aelian. ἀποσπ. 89; 98; 99;
100; 101. Aesch. in Anth. Gr. (ed.
Jacobs). Arist. Plut. 653–741.
Artemid. Oneir. V. 61; V. 89.
Athenae. I. 28 E. Callimach. 'Επιγ.
54; 55. Eudocia Aug. XI. Eustath.
ad. Δ 202. Galen. (ed. Kühn), Vol.
VI. pp. 41 and 869. Hipp. Rheg.
Frag. VIII. in Aelian. H. A. IX. 33.
Liban. Decl. XXXIX. Vol. I. 839 A.
Marin. Procl. 29. Paus. III. 19, 7;
III. 20, 5; X. 38, 13. Phylarch. Frag.
XVII. Polyanth. Frag. III. Suid.
art. 'Αρίσταρχος; Δομνῖνος; Παύσων.
Bau. 59; 60; 61; 80; 87. Bau.

Aus Epid. p. 13. CIG. 2292; 5980.
Philol. 1889, 401; 1890, 577. CIL.
III. 1, 1561.
Hand of Asklepios. Aelian. ἀποσπ.
99. Julian. Ep. 34, 406 D; 61,
450 A. Suid. art. Θεόπομπος.

SAVES FROM DANGER.

Aristid. 469. Paus. II. 10, 2. BCH.
II. pp. 86, 87. CIA. III. 1, Add.
et Corr. 132 b.

Oracle.

Aristid. 467, 12; 471, 24; 491, 16 ff.
Artemid. Oneir. IV. 22; V. 9;
V. 66. Herodian. IV. 8, 3. Jambl.
de Myst. III. 3. Liban. de Vit.
Sua. Vol. II. 48 A ff. Origen,
κατὰ Κελσ. III. 24. Paus. III. 23, 7;
X. 38, 13. Philost. Vit. Apoll. I. 9.
Max. Tyr. Diss. XV. 7. Bau. 59,
11; 80, 1, 23, 28, 51. Macrob.
Sat. I. 20, 4. Plaut. Curc. I. 1, 14.
κατὰ ὄναρ or ὄνειρον. Bau. 12; 37;
43; 46; 57; 61; 62; 97; 98; 99.
CIA. III. 1, Add. et Corr. 181 C.
CIG. 1176, 5. Le Bas, 145, 2.

Asklepios as Oath.

Julian. Orat. VII. 234 D. Menander,
Βοιωτ. (ed. Meinecke), Frag. IV.

Asklepios in Art.

Bearded.
Luc. Ζεὺς Τρ. 26. Paus. X. 34, 6.
Arnob. VI. 21. Cic. de Nat. Deor.
III. 34, 83. Lactant. de Or. Err.
4. Ovid, Met. XV. 656.
Youthful.
Paus. II. 10, 3; 13, 5; VIII. 25, 11;
28, 1; 32, 5. Anth. Pal. 3, 92, 19.
Fillets.
Luc. 'Αλεξ. 58.
Attributes.
Dog. Paus. II. 27, 2.
Pine cone. Paus. II. 10, 3.
Serpent. Paus. II. 27; 2.

Sceptre. Paus. II. 10, 3.

Staff. Cornut. p. 70, 33. Eudocia Aug. XI. Euseb. Praep. Ev. III. 11, 2. Hippoc. Ep. 13 (ed. Kühn, p. 778). Paus. II. 27, 2. Arnob. VI. 25. Ovid, Met. XV. 655.

Etymology.

Cornut. p. 70, 33. Etym. Gud. 'Aσκλ. Et. Mag. 'Aσκελέτ. Eudoc. Aug. XI. Eustath. ad Δ 202; ad Λ 518. Plut. Orat. Vit. VIII. Sch. Δ 195. Suid. art. Αἴγλη; Θεόπομπος; Παύσων. Macrob. Sat. I. 20. Bau. 84, 51.

SIGNIFICANCE OF ASKLEPIOS.

Julian. in Cyrill. c. Jul. VI. 200. Euseb. Praep. Ev. III. 11, 26; 13, 16. Paus. VII. 23, 8.

Temples.

Location.
Plut. Quaest. Rom. 94. Vitruv. I. 3, 7.

Trees.
Dion. Cass. 51, 8. Paus. II. 11, 6; III. 23, 7. Hippoc. Ep. 13 (ed. Kühn, p. 778). Bau. 59, 90, 121; 94.

Springs.
Aristid. 408 ff.; 486, 2 and 14. Arist. Plut. 656. Paus. I. 21, 4; II. 27, 5. 'Aθήν. V. 527, 10.

Outer Buildings.
Aristid. 447, 19; 449, 10 ff.; 473, 18; 506, 2. Paus. II. 4, 6; 11, 6; 27, 6 ff.; X. 32, 12. Porphyry, de Abstin. Anim. II. 17; cf. Coll. 3472. Bau. 60, 10. CIA. II. 1, Add. et Corr. 489 b. Coll. 3359.

Altars.
βωμός. Arist. Plut. 660. Eustath. ad B 561. Paus. III. 23, 7. Bau. 43; 68; 84, 28, 31. CIA. II. 3, 1443, 1650, 1651; III. 1, Add. et

Corr. 68 f. IGS. et I. 608; 1125. Kaibel, 800. Le Bas, II. 146 a. Philol. 1889, p. 401.
τρίβωμος. CIG. 5980.
ἐπιβόθρια. Aristid. 472, 11.
ἄδυτον. Bau. 80, 112; 84, 30.

Table.
Aristid. 495, 23; 516, 15. Athenae. XV. 693, 2. Sch. Arist. Plut. 678. CIA. II. 1, Add. Nov. 373 b; III. 1, Add. et Corr. 68 c.

Couch.
Paus. X. 32, 12. CIA. II. 1, Add. et Corr. 453 b, c.

Lamps.
Aristid. 447, 29; 541, 11. Arist. Plut. 668.

Treasury.
Bau. 87, 12.
Inventories. CIA. II. 2, 766; 767; 835; 836; 839; cf. 724; 725; 728; 737.

Animals in Cult.

Birds. Aelian. Var. Hist. V. 17; ἄποσπ. 98. Clem. Alex. protr. IV. 52. Paus. VIII. 25, 11.

Dogs. Aelian. H. A. VII. 13. Paus. II. 27, 2. Plut. de Sol. Anim. XIII. 11. Bau. 59, 126; 80, 35. Philol. 1890, p. 596. CIA. II. 3, 1651.

Serpents. Aelian. H. A. VIII. 12; XVI. 39. Arist. Plut. 732 ff. Cornut. p. 70, 33. Artemid. Oneir. II. 13. Eudocia Aug. XI. Herond. IV. 91. Hippoc. Ep. 17 (Kühn, p. 788). Paus. II. 11, 8; 28, 1; IX. 39, 3. Bau. 59, 113; 80, 118. Pliny, N. H. 29, 72. Stat. Silv. III. 4, 25.

Explanation of Serpent in Cult. Euseb. Praep. Ev. III. 11, 26. Macrob. Sat. I. 20, 1 ff.

Cult transferred by Serpent. Luc. 'Aλέξ. 13 ff. Paus. II. 10, 3;

III. 23, 7. Plut. Quaest. Rom. 94.
Arnob. VII. 44 ff. Augustin. de
Civ. Dei. X. 16, 36. Livy, X. 47;
XXIX. 11, 1; Ovid, Met. XV.
660 ff. Pliny, N. H. 29, 72.

Hierarchy. PRIEST.

Hereditary.
Aristid. 521, 12. Coll. 260. Philol.
1890, p. 578. Cf. p. 583.
Chosen.
Ross, Inscr. Ined. II. 221.
By Lot. CIA. II. 1, Add. et Corr.
489 *b*; Add. Nov. 352 *b*; 567 *b*.
Paton and Hicks, Inscr. of Cos,
n. 103 (?).
By Oracle. CIA. II. 3, 1654.
By Purchase. Coll. 3052.
Term of Office.
Year. Bau. 6, *a*, *b*; 60; 61. BCH.
I. p. 161, n. 24; p. 168, n. 83; II.
p. 86; VI. p. 498. CIA. II. 1,
Add. et Corr. 453, *b*, *c*; 489, *b*; II.
2, 835; 836; II. 3, 1204; 1440;
1446–48; 1456; 1459–61; 1466;
1468; 1472; 1473; 1475; 1476;
1479; 1481; 1483; 1489–91; 1495;
1496; 1505; 1511; III. 1, 99; 131;
144; 228; 229; 693; Add. et Corr.
68 *a*, *b*; 132 *n*, *o*; 181 *h*; 228 *a*, *b*;
229 *a*, *b*. Coll. 3025. Ditt. 439.
Mitth. d. Arch. Inst. VIII. 103.
Life. BCH. V. 474; XII. 88. CIA.
III. 1, 132; Add. et Corr. 68 *a*, *b*;
132 *o*; 229 *a*; 712 *a*. Coll. 260.
Paton and Hicks, Inscr. of Cos, n.
92. Ross, Inscr. Ined. II. 221.
εἰσι[τη]ρήρια. CIA. II. 1, Add. et Corr.
453 *b*, *c*.
Duties of Priest. Ἀθήν. VI. p. 134, n. 9.
Arist. Plut. 676.
Care of Temple. CIA. II. 1, Add.
et Corr. 453 *b*, *c*; 489 *b*; Add.
Nov. 373 *b*; 567 *b*; 477 *b*, *c*. Coll.
1532 *a*, *b*; 1548 *a*, *b*; 3052.

Sacrifices. Herond. IV. 87 ff. Bau.
1; 24; 37–42; 47; 53; 57; 57 *a*;
58; 62; 63; 67; 68; 73; 97.
CIA. II. 1, Add. et Corr. 453 *b*, *c*;
Add. Nov. 373 *b*; 477 *b*–567 *b*; II.
3, 1204; III. 1, Add. et Corr.
102 *a*, *b*. CIG. 1175; 2428. Ditt.
378. Coll. 3327. IGS. et I. 2283.
Reports. CIA. II. 1, Add. Nov.
373 *b*; 477 *b*.
Public Honors.
CIA. II. 1, Add. et Corr. 453 *b*; Add.
Nov. 373 *b*; 477 *b*, *c*; 567 *b*; III. 1,
263; 287. Coll. 3052.

NEOCORE.

Herond. IV. 40; 45; 90. Aelian.
H. A. VII. 13.
Term of Office.
CIA. III. 1, Add. et Corr. 132 *o*;
181 *c*, *f*, *h*; 229 *b*; 231 *a*, *b*; 774 *a*, *b*;
780 *a*, *b*; 894 *a*.
Number.
Aristid. 473, 5; 477, 14. Coll. 255.
Duties.
Aristid. 447, 29; 474, 12; 494, 14.
CIA. III. 1, Add. et Corr. 68 *c*, *e*, *f*.
Philol. 1890, p. 587.
Sacrifices. CIA. III. 1, 68, 102; Add.
et Corr. 68 *e*, *f*; 171 *a*; 780 *b*.
Public Honors.
CIA. III. 1, 780; Add. et Corr.
780 *a*, *b*, *c*.

ὑποζάκορος.

CIA. III. 1, Add. et Corr. 894 *a*.

κλειδοῦχος.

CIA. II. 1, Add. et Corr. 453 *b*, *c*; II.
3, 1204; III. 1, Add. et Corr. 102 *a*;
712 *a*; 780 *a*.

FIRE LIGHTER.

Bau. 5, 1; 6 *a*, *b*; 8; 49; 50; 55;
69; 72. CIA. III. 1, 693. Coll.
3327; 3359.

Μάγιρος.

Bau. 101.

ἰαροργός.

Philol. 1890, p. 587.

ἱεροκῆρυξ.

CIA. III. 1, Add. et Corr. 780 *a*.

Ἀσκληπιασταί.

CIA. II. 1, Add. et Corr. 617 *b*.

Ὀργεῶνες.

CIA. II. 2, 990.

MEDICAL ASSISTANTS.

Aristid. 447, 26; 477, 15; Arist. Plut. 701; 710. Bau. 59, 114; 80, 12, 40, 113.

ἀῤῥηφόρος.

CIA. II. 1, Add. et Corr. 453 *b*.

κανηφόρος.

CIA. II. 3, 1204; III. 1, Add. et Corr. 920 *a*.

Private Ritual.

Bathing.
Arist. Plut. 656. Bau. 60, 12.

Mattress.
Arist. Plut. 663.

Sleeping.
Arist. Plut. 662 ff. Paus. II. 27, 2. Plaut. Curc. I. 1, 14.

In ἄβατον. Bau. 59, 4, 21, 50, 63, 65, 109, 116, 117; 60, 19; 80, 23, 25, 44, 49, 51, 102.

In ἐγκοιμητήριον. Bau. 61, 7.

In πρόδομος. Suid. art. Δομνῖνος.

In τέμενος. Bau. 80, 11.

At Night.
Aristid. 474, 5. Arist. Vesp. 123. Artemid. Oneir. V. 9. Jambl. de Myst. III. 3. Cic. de Divin. II. 59. Bau. 59, 4, 25, 37, 49, 57, 68,

76, 93, 98, 107, 124; 73; 80, 9, 16, 23, 27, 39, 46, 58, 66, 69, 88, 103, 111, 117, 120, 123.

Sacrifices.
Aristid. 64, 2; 472, 16; 500, 7. Arist. Plut. 660; cf. Sch. *ibid.* Artemid. Oneir. II. 33; V. 9; V. 66. Herond. IV. 12. Liban. Decl. XXXIX, 842 A ff. Paus. II. 10, 3; 27, 4; III. 19, 7; X. 38, 13. Philost. Vit. Soph. 266, V. Plato, Phaedo, 118 A. Suid. art. Ἀρίσταρχος. Tertul. Ad. Nat. II. 2. Theophrast. Char. 21. Bau. 52; 55; 59, 38, 42, 45, 56, 60, 70, 89, 93; 60, 13, 20; 87, 8, 35, 38, 82, 101. BCH. III. p. 193. CIA. II. 1, 470, l. 17, 55; III. 1, 132; Add. et Corr. 132 *a-i*; 132 *l-o*; 132 *r*. CIG. 2429; 5975. IGS. et I. 967; 968; 2283.

Animal Sacrifice.
Consumed within precinct. Paus. II. 27, 1. Ditt. 378.

Cock. Artemid. Oneir. V. 9; Herond. IV. 12. Liban. Decl. XXXIX. 842 A. Luc. Δὶς Κατ. 5. Plato, Phaedo, 118 A. Tertul. Ad. Nat. II. 2.

Geese. Aristid. 500, 7.

Goat. Paus. II. 26, 9; X. 32, 12. Sex. Emp. Pyrrh. hyp. 3, 221. Servius ad Verg. Georg. II. 380.

Pig. Paus. II. 11, 7. Sext. Emp. Pyrrh. hyp. 3, 220.

Ram. Paus. II. 11, 7.

Steles.
Aristid. 38, 14. Paus. II. 27, 3 ff.; 36, 1. Strab. VIII. 6, 15; XIV. 2, 20. Pliny, N. H. 29, 4.

Fines paid to Asklepios.
BCH. X. 358. Coll. 304 *b*; 1532 *a*, *b*; 1547; 1548 *a*, *b*; 3052.
For enslaving. BCH. X. 378 ff.; Coll. 1447; 1532; 1545; 1548. Ditt. 445.

Slaves dedicated.
Coll. 811; 1474; 1546. Sueton. de
Vit. Caes. V. 25.

Physicians sacrifice.
CIA. II. 1, Add. Nov. 352 *b*. Cf. II.
3, 1449. IGS. et I. 689; 967 *a*,
b; 2283. CIL. II. 21.
Honored. CIA. II. 1, Add. Nov.
256 *b*.

• **Public Ritual.**

FESTIVALS.

Asklepieia. Aristid. 124, 1. Dion.
Cass. 47, 2. Pollux, I. 37. Steph.
Byz. art. Καπετώλιον. BCH. IV.
p. 378. CIG. 1165; 1429; 1515
a, *b*; 1715; 3208. Coll. 1232;
4315. IGGS. 18.
Agrigentum. Mionn. I. 214, 53.
Ankyra. BCH. IX. p. 69. CIG.
3428; 4016; 4017. Mionn. IV.
384, 62.
Athens. Aesch. Ctes. p. 455. CIA.
II. 2, 741; II. 3, 1367.
Epidauros. Paus. II. 26, 8. Pind.
Nem. III. 145; Sch. *ibid.* Plato,
Ion 530 A. Bau. 10; 32; 84, 10–
26; 94. CIG. 1171; 1186; 3208;
5913. Coll. 3290. Ditt. 398, 4.
IGGS. 49. Mionn. II. 238, 63 and
64; S IV. 260.
Karpathos. Rev. Arch. 1863, p. 470,
l. 23.
Kos. Hippoc. Ep. 13 (ed. Kühn,
p. 778). BCH. V. p. 211, n. 6;
p. 213. Ditt. 398, 13; 399. Paton
and Hicks, Inscr. of Cos, n. 14, l. 7.
Lampsakos. CIG. 3641 *b*.
Laodikeia. Head, 566.
Nikaia. Head, 443.
Pergamon. Mitth. d. Arch. Inst.
XVI. p. 132.
Rhodiopolis. CIG. 4315 n.
Soli. Q. Curtius Rufus. Hist. Alex.
III. 7, 3.
Thyateira. BCH. X. 415, 24.
Tyre. Head, 676.

Epidauria.
Paus. II. 26, 8. Philost. Vit. Apoll.
IV. 18, p. 72. CIA. II. 1, Add. et
Corr. 453 *b*; III. 1, 916.
Heroia.
CIA. II. 1, Add. et Corr. 453 *b*, *c*.
πανήγυρις.
Hippoc. Ep. 13 (ed. Kühn, p. 778).
Bau. 10. BCH. V. p. 211, n. 6,
17; p. 213.
παννυχίς.
CIA. II. 1, Add. et Corr. 453 *b*, *c*;
Add. Nov. 373 *b*.
Vintage Festival.
Arnob. VII. 32.
Procession.
Hippoc. Ep. 13 (Kühn, p. 778). CIA.
III. 1, 921. Bau. 84.

DRESS.

Appian, Lib. 130. Aristid. 473, 8;
494, 6. Bau. 84, 19.

INCENSE.

Aristid. 64, 21. Philost. Vit. Soph.
p. 266, l. 25.

SINGING.

Aelian, ἀποσπ. 98. Aristid. 479, 11;
cf. Sch. Arist. Plut. 636; 513, 9;
514, 17; 517, 28. Galen. (ed. Kühn),
Vol. VI. p. 41. Marin. Procl.
19. Paus. III. 26, 10. Suid. art.
ἀσκωλίαζε.

Pæans.
Aristid. 453, 4. Athenae. VI. 250 *c*.
· Luc. Δημ. ἐγκώμ. 27. Philost. Vit.
Apoll. III. 17, p. 50. Philost. Jun.
Imag. 13, p. 17. Bau. 84, 31 ff.
CIA. III. 1, 171; Add. et Corr.
171 *b*, *c*, *d*, *g*, *k*. CIG. 3538;
5973 *c*. Rev. Arch. 1889, p. 71.

PUBLIC SACRIFICES.

Aristid. 448, 18; 531, 8. Paus. II. 11,
7. Polyb. 32, 27, 2 ff. CIA. II, 1,
Add. et Corr. 453 *b*, *c*; III. 1, 1159;

Add. et Corr. 77 a. CIG. 3538; 5980.

DECREES DEPOSITED IN THE ASKLEPIEION.

BCH. V. p. 211, n. 6, l. 19. CIA. II. 1, Add. Nov. 256 *b*; 373 *b*;

477 *b*; 567 *b*; II. 2, 840. Coll. 361 ; 3430 ; 3462. Ditt. 439. Mitth. d. Arch. Inst. XI. p. 263. Paton and Hicks, Inscr. of Cos, 14.

ἱερὰ γερουσία τοῦ Ἀσκ.

IGGS. 2808.

LOCALITY OF CULTS.

A geographical classification has been made in the following list of Asklepieia, as that seems more satisfactory than an historical arrangement which could at best be only approximately accurate. An attempt, however, is made to indicate the development of the cult, and to show that to a great extent the historical and geographical groups coincide.

Literary and epigraphical sources furnish us with information of about 207 Asklepieia, but the names of the remaining 161 are only known by coins which bear one or more of the types of Asklepios, Hygieia or Telesphoros. The existence of such coins, however, is no proof of the worship of Asklepios at any given locality. Most of them were struck under the Emperors, and the designs may have been merely transferred from one town to another, as in the case of coins bearing the image of the Ephesian Artemis, which are found in too many of the neighboring towns to admit of the supposition of a similar cult-statue in each. Also, alliance coins may bear the figure of a god of one town who is unknown in the other. Or a coin design may simply be the arms of the town. The probability is that the cult existed in a large proportion of the towns where the Asklepios coins are found, but no one can determine with certainty in which town, unless additional material comes to hand. A few towns are mentioned in which statues or reliefs have been found or alluded to. Such evidence is less satisfactory even than that of the coins.

THESSALY.

As has already been shown, the oldest seat of the Asklepios cult was in Thessaly. The ordinary type of Asklepios standing with serpent and staff is used on coins of the country as a whole.

Catalogue of Coins in the British Museum, Thessaly, 6.

Atrax. Coins of the third century B.C.

Head, 249.

Kierion. Coins of the first half of the fourth century. Asklepios *adolescens* or Apollo with the serpent. If it is Asklepios, it is the earliest representation on coins.

Head, 249.

Krannon. Decree posted in the Asklepieion.   Coll. 361 A.

Lakereia. The local legends of Koronis point to a cult of Asklepios here, but there is no further evidence.

Larissa. Coins : A. feeds serpent; head of A. with serpent.   B. M. Thess. 28. Head, 255.

Phalanna. Dedications to A.   Coll. 1329; 1332.
    Decrees dated by priest of A.   Mitth. d. Arch. Inst. VIII. 103 and 107.

Pherai. Dedication to A.   Coll. 338.

Pharsalos. Dedication to A.   Coll. 329.

Trikka. The two sons of A. led the forces from T. to Troy.   B 729; Δ 202. Eustath. ad B 729.
    Here was the birthplace of the god,[1] and his oldest and most famous shrine.[2] Cures were here recorded.[3]   [1] Strab. XIV. 1, 39. [2] Strab. IX. 5, 17; VIII. 4, 4. Herond. IV. 1. [3] Strab. VIII. 6, 15.
    Coin of the first half of the fourth century; A. seated, feeding serpent with a bird.   B. M. Thess. 52.

Iolkos. Dedication to A. and Hygieia.   Mitth. d. Arch. Inst. XV. 304.

MAGNESIA.

The spread of the cult from Thessaly is natural, and there are Magnesian coins in München which show the god seated. A serpent on a coin from *Homolion* may symbolize the god.   Head, 252 and 256.

EPEIROS.

Ambrakia. Temple of A.   Polyb. XXI. 27, 2.

Nikopolis. Coins : A. stands with or without staff entwined by serpent; is seated feeding serpent as on the coin of Trikka; stands in temple.   Mionn. S III. 372–410.

KORKYRA.

Specifications for temple.   Coll. 3195.
Coins : A. stands with serpent-staff.   Mionn. II. 76, 75.

AKARNANIA.

Anaktorion. Dedication to A.   Coll. 1385 b.

LOKRIS OZOLIS.

Amphissa. Slave freed and dedicated to A.   Coll. 1474.

Naupaktos. Ruined temple which had been erected in gratitude for a cure.

Paus. X. 38, 13.

Slaves freed and dedicated.

Mitth. d. Arch. Inst. IV. p. 22 ff.

PHOKIS.

The cult was brought from Thessaly at an early date by the Phlegyans to Phokis where Asklepios was throughout the entire country worshiped as tribal god, ἀρχαγέτηѕ. Here the conflict took place between the gods of the invading tribe and Apollo, which resulted in a close connection of divinities in myth and cult.

Paus. X. 32, 12.

Drymaia. Dedication to A.

Coll. 1530.

Elateia. Fines paid to A.

Coll. 1532 a, b, c.

Dedication to A. and Hygieia.

BCH. X. 358.

Temple and bearded statue by Timokles and Timarchides.

Paus. X. 34, 6.

Panopeus. Statue of A. said to be Prometheus.

Paus. X. 4, 4.

Stiris. Fines paid to A.

Coll. 1545; 1547; 1548 a, b.

Dedications to A.

Coll. 1541; 1542.

Tithorea. Seventy stadia distant from T. is a temple of A. ἀρχαγέτης. Within the enclosure are the houses for suppliants and attendants of the god, and in the middle stands the temple and a bearded statue of stone, over two feet high. A couch is at the right of the image. All kinds of sacrifices are offered here except goats.

Paus. X. 32, 12.

BOEOTIA.

The worship of Asklepios in Boeotia is very old, brought by the wandering tribes of Thessaly. In Boeotia is a confusion between this god and Trophonios to whom the same ancestry is given[1] and whose representations are similar.[2]

[1] Cic. de Nat. Deor. III. 22, 56.
[2] Paus. IX. 39, 4.

Hyettos. Sacred council of A.

IGGS. 2808.

Orchomenos. List of contributors to temple of A.

Coll. 474; 475.

Tanagra. Cure by means of a cock.

Aelian. ἀποσπ. 98.

Statuette of A.

Mitth. d. Arch. Inst. III. 395, n. 171.

Thespiai. Dedications to A.

IGGS. 1779; Ditt. 1824.

Slave dedicated and stele placed in temple.

Coll. 811.

Thisbe. Dedication to A.

Coll. 747 a.

ATTICA.

Acharnai. Temple of A.

Sch. Arist. Plut. 621.

Athens. So much of the material derived from Athens has been already discussed in the main body of this work, that it is inadvisable to repeat it in the index.

The cult was introduced into Athens in the fifth century together with Aphrodite Pandemos and Themis, whose shrines lay in the enclosure of Asklepios in Epidauros, and were near by on the south slope of the Acropolis at Athens. The date of the founding of the cult is not sure. According to Wilamowitz it was about the year 460 B.C., though tradition of Asklepios in relation to Sophocles would place it much later. The earliest mention of the cult is by Hermippos in the Scholia of the Plutos, line 701. The temple was still in existence in the fifth century A.D.[1]

There were several Asklepieia in Athens. Two temples were built on the Acropolis site,[2] the second not replacing the first, but built near it. The Orgeones held a sanctuary in the deme of Prospalta[3] and there was still another shrine within the city.[4] In Peiraeus was an Asklepieion which is directly mentioned but once, though the expression "the temple in the city," which is used in reference to the one on the Acropolis, may imply that the temple in Peiraeus was at one time equally important.[5] Pausanias and Xenophon both spoke of the water facilities in the Asklepieion on the Acropolis[6] and the grove and the elevation did something to render the location a health-giving one.

Many inscriptions and reliefs come from Athens, so that we know more in regard to the cult here than in any other locality. For the most part these inscriptions are to be found in the collection of Attic inscriptions in the second and third divisions. Those which bear directly on the cult are the following: CIA. II. 1, 470; Add. et Corr. 162; 453 *b, c*; 489 *b*; Add. Nov. 159 *b*; 256 *b*; 352 *b*; 373 *b*; 477 *b, c*; 567 *b*; II. 2, 724; 725; 728; 737; 741; 766; 767; 835; 836; 839; 840; II. 3, 1204; 1440–1511; 1649–1651; 1654; III. 1, 68; 99; 102; 132; 144; 163; 171; 181–184; 228; 229; 263; 287; 693; 729; 780; 781; 916; 921; 1159; Add. et Corr. 65 *a*; 68 *a–f*; 77 *a*;

[1] Marin. Procl. 29.

[2] CIA. II. 1, Add. et Corr. 489 *b*; Add. Nov. 159 *b*; 477 *b*.

[3] CIA. II. 2, 990.

[4] Ditt. 378.

[5] Sch. Arist. Plut. 621. Cf. CIA. II. 1, Add. Nov. 159*b*; 477 *b*.

[6] Paus. I. 21, 4; Xen. Mem. 3, 13, 3.

102 *a–c*; 132 *a–r*; 171 *a–k*; 181 *a–h*; 184 *a*; 185 *a–c*;
228 *a*, *b*; 229 *a*, *b*; 231 *a*, *b*; 411 *a*; 712 *a*; 713 *a*;
774 *a*, *b*; 780 *a*, *b*, *c*; 836 *c*; 894 *a*. For others from
the Asklepieion not bearing the name, see III. 1,
p. 494 ff.

References to the Athenian cult which have not
been elsewhere discussed are these: Arist. Vesp. 123.
Luc. Ἁλιεύς, 42; Δημ. Βίος, 27; Ἑρμότ. 37; Ἰκαρομ.
16. Paus. I. 21, 4 ff. Suid. art. Δομνῖνος.

Coins, 186–146 B.C.: A. and Hygieia; A. standing
with serpent-staff.

Head. p. 321; 324; 327. Mionn. II. 124, 140 and 141.

MEGARIS.

Megara. A statue of A. and Hygieia of Bryaxis.
    Coins: A. and Hygieia.

Paus. I. 40, 6.
B. M. Attica, 123.

Pagai. Coins: A. and Isis.

Jour. Hell. Stud. VIII. 50.

KORINTHOS.

Kenchreiai. Temple of A. near one of Isis.

Paus. II. 2, 3.

Korinthos. Temple of A. with statues of A. and
Hygieia in white stone.
    Coins: A. and Hygieia standing; Hygieia feeding
serpent from patera; A. standing.

Paus. II. 4, 5.
Mionn. II. 184, 270; II. 189, 308; S IV. 102, 693; S IV. 113, 771.

Sikyon. The god in the form of a serpent was brought
from Epidauros by a woman of Sikyon, Nikagora
by name. A figure of Hypnos lies in the outer
court of the temple, and within is a shrine of Apollo
Karneios. In the stoa lie the bones of a whale, and
statues of Oneiros, and Hypnos lulling a lion to
sleep. Images of Pan and Artemis stand on either
side of the entrance. The beardless statue of A.,
chryselephantine, the work of Kalamis, holds a
sceptre and a pinecone. The Sikyonians consider
Aratos the son of A.
    A trophy is placed in temple of A.
    Coins: Hygieia standing; A. standing.

Paus. II. 10, 2 ff.
Paus. IV. 14, 8.
Athenae. VIII. 351, f.
Mionn. II. 201, 382; S IV. 170, 1131.

Titane. The cult of A. in Titane is one of the oldest
in Peloponnesos. Here Pausanias saw a very ancient
cult-statue, muffled, so as to show only the head
and the hands and feet. A similar image of
Hygieia was nearly hidden from view by the locks of

hair hung upon it by suppliant women.¹ The cult
was of Thessalian origin as is shown both by its
being founded by Alexanor, son of Machaon, and
the presence of Koronis, whose statue was carried
into the sanctuary of Athena to receive a share of
the sacrifices. Alexanor and Euamerion have here
a double cult, the first as hero, the second as god.
Pausanias identifies the latter as Telesphoros of the
Pergamene cult, and Akesis of the Epidaurian.

The temple stood in a grove of cypress, above
which were the houses for the suppliants.² The
sacrifice of animals took place on the ground, except
in the case of birds, which were burned on the altar.³
No portion of the offerings could be carried out of
the enclosure.⁴

Dedication to A.

¹ Cf. Paus. VII. 23, 8.

² Paus. II. 11, 6 ff.

³ Paus. II. 11, 7.

⁴ Paus. II. 27, 1.
BCH. III. 193.

PHLIASIA.

Phlious. Coming down from the Acropolis, a temple of
A. stood on the right. The statue was beardless.

Coins : A. standing.

Paus. II. 13, 5.

Mionn. II. 198, 368; S IV.
159, 1044. Head, 345.

ARGOLIS.

The cults in Argolis spread from the centre of the
Asklepios worship, Epidauros. They are numerous
and the ritual is highly developed.

Argos. Sphyros, a son of Machaon and brother of
Alexanor, is said to have founded the cult. The
cult-statue was of white stone, showing the god
seated and Hygieia standing near. The statues were
by Xenophilos and Straton.

Two other shrines are mentioned by Pausanias.

Coins: A. seated presenting some object to serpent, the type of the statue of Epidauros.

Paus. II. 23, 4.

Paus. II. 21, 1; 23, 2.
Mionn. S IV. 51, 103. Head,
368.

Asine. Coins: A. standing.

Mionn. II. 224, 73; S IV. 257,
132.

Epidauros. As in the treatment of Athens and for
the same reasons, only such material is given here as
is not to be found in the body of the text.

This town was the special seat of the Asklepios
cult⁵ until the Pergamene cult eclipsed it. The god
frequently bears the name Epidaurius, in Greek or
Latin,⁶ and the Epidaurians held their city sacred to
him.⁷ They claimed that he was born here and

⁵ Herond. IV. 2. Julian. in
Cyr. Alex. c. Jul. VI. 200.
Strab. VIII. 6, 15.
⁶ Clem. Alex. protr. IV. 53;
Arnob. III. 21; Cic. de
Nat. Deor. III. 34, 83.
⁷ Eustath. ad B 561; Suid.
art. Ἐπίδαυρος. Minuc.
Fel. 6, 1.

called the headlands by the town by his name.[1]
Besides the main Asklepieion, there was a τέμενος
with statues of A. and Epione in the city itself.[2]

The cult-statue, which is known only by descrip-
tions and coins, was the work of Thrasymedes.
Athenagoras mentioned one of Phidias which was
at Epidauros.[3] Pausanias mentions the fact that
this statue which was placed over a cistern, ἐπὶ
φρέατι, received different treatment from that of
other statues, as neither oil nor water was used to
cleanse it.[4] The statue was the sufferer from a
joke of Dionysius, who took off its golden beard,
on the plea that a beardless father should not have
a bearded son.[5] The temple was further despoiled
by Sulla,[6] though in later times the Romans did
much for the improvement of the sanctuary,[7] especially under Antoninus.

The cult in Epidauros is mentioned casually by
many authors. Most of the references have already
been given. These should be added : Arrian, Anab.
VII. 14, 6; Hippol. Omn. Hoer. Ref. IV. 32;
Pliny, N. H. IV. 18; Plut. Pomp. 24; Porphyry, de
Abstin. Anim. II. 17. Stat. Silv. I. 4, 61 ff.

Coins : A. seated; A. standing; head of A.;
Hygieia with serpent; child, goat and shepherd.
Many coins bear Ἀσκλήπια, in honor of the festivals
which were here most important.

Hermione. Dedications to A.
 Festival of A.

Kleone. Coins: A. seated.

Lessa. Enclosure of A. mentioned.

Troizen. A statue of A. by Timotheos, which the
people call Hippolytos.
 Enclosure mentioned.
 Coins : A. standing before altar with patera and
serpent-staff.

ACHAIA.

Aigion. Enclosure of A. and Hygieia mentioned.
 Coins : A. standing.

Aigeira. Statue of A. in temple of Apollo.
 Coins : Crowned head of A.; A. standing.

Araxos. Ivory image of A.

[1] Eurip. Hipp. 1209.

[2] Paus. II. 29, 1.

[3] Athenag. πρεσβ. ch. 17.

[4] Paus. V. 11, 11.

[5] Cic. de Nat. Deor. III. 34, 83. Lactant. de Or. Er. IV.
[6] Diodor. 38, 7.
[7] Paus. II. 27, 6. Strab. XII. 5, 3.

Mionn. II. 237, 59–73; S IV. 260–261. Panofka, Tf. I. 1.

CIG. 1221 ; 1222.
CIG. 1165 ; 1186. Coll. 3396.

Head, 369.

Coll. 3361.

Paus. II. 32, 4.

Bau. 80, 10.
Mionn. S IV. 268, 196.

Paus. VII. 23, 7.
Mionn. S IV. 29, 166.

Paus. VII. 26, 6.
Mionn. II. 164, 118; S IV. 22, 129.

Strab. VIII. 3, 4.

Kyros. A sanctuary of A. with abundant water. The image is by the largest spring.   Paus. VII. 27, 11.

This cult may have come directly from Thessaly.   Curtius, Pel. 1, 484.

Olenos. Sanctuary of A. mentioned.   Strab. VII. 4.

Patrai. A sanctuary of A. above the Acropolis.   Paus. VII. 21, 14.
    Coins: A. standing.   B. M. Pelop. 28.

Pellene. Coins: A. standing.   Mionn. S IV. 157, 1038; 158, 1041.

ARKADIA.

Aliphera. Hieron of A. mentioned.   Paus. VIII. 26, 6.

Gortys. A marble temple of A. was standing in the time of Pausanias. The cult-statue was beardless, and this as well as a statue of Hygieia was the work of Skopas. Alexander had dedicated his shield and spear here.   Paus. VIII. 28, 1.

Heraia. Dedication to sons of A.   BCH. III. 190.

Kaphyai. Coin: A. standing.   Jour. Hell. Stud. VII. 104.

Kaus. Forty stadia from Thelpusa was a sanctuary of A. Καούσιος.   Paus. VIII. 25, 1.

Kleitor. Hieron of A.   Paus. VIII. 21, 3.
    Coins: A. standing.   Mionn. S IV. 277, 35.

Mantineia. A double temple of A. and of Leto with her children. The statue of A. was the work of Alkamenes.   Paus. VIII. 9, 1.
    Decree from the priests of A.   Le Bas, 352 *j.*
    A statuette of Telesphoros has been found here.   BCH. XIV. 595 ff.
    Coins: A. standing; Hygieia.   Mionn. II. 249, 33, 35; II. 249, 34.

Megalopolis. Statues of A. and Hygieia at the entrance of the sanctuary of the Great Goddesses. There were two sanctuaries of A., in the second of which the god was honored as Παῖς. The image was but a cubit high.   Paus. VIII. 31. 1.
    Paus. VIII. 32, 4 ff.
    Dedication to A. and Hygieia.   BCH. VI. 194.

Orchomenos. Coins: A. standing.   Mionn. II. 251, 48; S IV. 283, 66.

Phigalea. Coins: A. standing.   Mionn. II. 253, 56, 60; S IV. 289, 94, 98.

Tegea. Statues of A. and Hygieia, by Skopas.   Paus. VIII. 47, 1.
    Temple and statue of A. on road to Argos.   Paus. VIII. 54, 5.

Aristarchos of Tegea was cured.

Relief of Asklepios.

Thelpusa.   Temple of A. in the town.

The localization of a tradition of the exposure and rescue of the infant Asklepios similar to the one of Epidauros together with the cult of A. Παῖς in a second sanctuary is evidence for an early established cult.

ELIS.

Kyllene.   Statue of A.

Olympia.   Statues of A. and Hygieia.

Forty stadia from the ridge of *Sauros* was a temple of A.

ZAKYNTHOS.

Coins: A. standing.

MESSENIA.

The Messenian cult claims not to be derived, but to be independent of either Thessalian or Epidaurian traditions.   The recurrence here of the town names Trikka, Ithome and Oichalia led to the tradition of the early connection of A. and his sons with Messenia, and the legends concerning the Messenian ancestry of the god.   It is, however, probable that the cult was imported directly from Thessaly at an early date.   Thraemer suggests a confusion between A. and some similar deity of the Leukippidae.

Coins of the country bear the standing god.

Abia.   Sanctuary of A.

Asine.   Coin: A. standing.

Gerenia.   The sanctuary of A. Τρικκαῖος was a model of the one at Trikka.

Here was a monument of Machaon.

Korone.   A temple and statue of A.

Kyparissiai, the port of Messene, had a temple and statue of A. Αὐλώνιος.

Coins: A. standing.

Aelian. ἄποσπ. 101. Suid. art. 'Αρίστ.
Mitth. d. Arch. Inst. IV. 137, 35.
Paus. VIII. 25, 3.
Paus. VIII. 25, 11.

Strab. VIII. 3, 4.

Paus. V. 20, 3 ; 26, 2.

Paus. VI. 21, 4.

Head, 360. Mionn. S IV. 199, 47 ; 202, 68.

Mionn. S II. 212, 31.

Paus. IV. 30, 1.

Head, 362.

Strab. VIII. 4, 4.

Paus. IV. 3, 2.

Paus. IV. 34, 6.

Paus. IV. 36, 7.

Head, 362.

Messene. Sanctuary of A. containing statues of the god and his sons, and of other deities, among whom Apollo should be noticed. Paus. IV. 31, 10.

Coins : A. standing. Head, 362.

Pylos. Coins : A. standing. Head, 363.

Thuria. Coins: A. standing. Head, 363.

LAKONIA.

The Lakonian cult is in close relation to the Messenian.

Asopos. Twelve stadia above Asopos was a sanctuary of A. where the god had the epithet Φιλόλαος. Paus. III. 22, 9.

Fifty stadia away was another sanctuary, called *Hyperteleaton.* Paus. III. 22, 10.

Boiai. A temple of A., Serapis and Isis was in the Agora, and a sanctuary of A. and Hygieia seven stadia distant. Paus. III. 22, 13.

Coins : A. standing. Mionn. II. 225, 79; S IV. 229, 52.

Brasiai. A sanctuary of A. Paus. III. 24, 5.

Epidauros Limera. The cult was founded on account of the escape here of a serpent which was being carried from Epidauros to Kos. Here were altars and an olive grove. Paus. III. 23, 7.

A Hieron of A. is in the town itself. Paus. III. 23, 10.

Gytheion. Statue of A. stands in a roofless temple. Paus. III. 21, 8.

Coins : A. standing in shrine which has a roof only over the back part; A. sacrificing at altar before which is serpent. B. M. Pelop. 133. Mionn. II. 226, 82; S IV. 231, 62; 232, 66; 233, 74.

Priest of A. mentioned. CIG. 1392.

Altar to A. Ὑπηκόῳ. S. Reinach, Chroniques d'Orient, p. 395. Cf. Wide, Lakon. Kult. p. 183. CIG. 1444.

Helos. Cult of A. Σχοινᾶτας. Paus. III. 24, 8.

Hypsoi. Sanctuary of A. Paus. III. 24, 8.

Kyphanta. Sanctuary and statue of A. Paus. III. 24, 2.

Las. Besides the shrine on the mountains called Hypsoi was a temple of A. on the summit of another ridge. Paus. III. 24, 8.

Coins: A. standing; Hygieia feeding serpent. Mionn. S IV. 234, 78, 79. Head, 365.

Leuktra. A. had great honor in Leuktra. Pausanias mentions a cult-statue. Paus. III. 26, 4.

Pellana. Sanctuary of A.   Paus. III. 21, 2.

Sparta. A. had several shrines in the neighborhood
of Sparta.[1] On the way to Therapne is a temple of   [1] Paus. III. 14, 2; 14, 7; 15,
A. Κοτυλεύς, built by Herakles because in his con-   10.
flict with Hippokoön and sons he received a wound
on the hip, κοτύλη.[2]   [2] Paus. III. 19, 7.
     Coins : A. standing ; Hygieia.   Head, 365

Therai. Herakles cured by A.   Paus. III. 20, 5.

MOESIA.

Anchialos. Coins : A. standing.   Head, 236. Mionn. S II. 215–228.

Dionysopolis. Coins : Hygieia with serpent.   Head, 234.

Marcianopolis. Coins : A. standing ; Telesphoros   Mionn. I. 358, 34 ; S II. 82–
standing ; Hygieia feeding serpent.   110.

Nikopolis. Coins : A. standing ; A., Hygieia and   Mionn. S II. 118–179.
Telesphoros ; Hygieia feeding serpent.

Tomi. Coins : A. standing ; Hygieia feeding serpent.   Mionn. S. II. 185–204.

NORTH OF BLACK SEA.

Hagion. A. mentioned.   Alex. Polyhist. Frag. 38.

Pantikapaion. Mentioned.   Strab. II. 11, 16.
     Coins : Head of A.; A. standing.   Mionn. S II. 11, 66.

DALMATIA.

Narona. Dedications to A. and Hygieia.   CIL. III. 1, 1766–1768.

Salona. Dedication to A.   CIL. III. 1, 1934.

PANNONIA INFERIOR.

Aquincum. Dedication to A. and Hygieia.   CIL. III. 1, 3412, 3413.

Campona. Dedication to A. and Hygieia.   CIL. III. 1, 3388.

Intercisa. Dedications to A. and Hygieia in Latin and   CIL. III. 1, 3326.
Greek.

Salva. Dedication to A. and Hygieia.   CIL. III. 1, 3649.

PANNONIA SUPERIOR.

Julia Emona. Dedication to A.   CIL. III. 1, 3834.

NORICUM.

Virinum. Dedication to A. and Hygieia. CIL. III. 2, 4772.

DACIA.

Also-Ilosva. Dedications to A. and Hygieia in Latin and Greek. CIL. III. 1, 786.

Ampelum. Dedications to A. ·
In the district *Apulum* inscriptions have been found in several towns. CIL. III. 1, 1278-1280.

Alba Julia. Dedications to *Numen Aesculapii; Numen Salutis;* to *Aures Aesculapii, Apollonis, Dianae;* to A. and Hygieia and other gods of health. CIL. III. 1, 972; 976; 978; 982-984; 986; 987. CIG. 6815.

Carlsburg. Priest of A. dedicates to Serapis; dedications to A. and Hygieia; to the Carthaginian gods and A. CIL. III. 1, 973-975; 977; 981; 985; 993.

In at least two different places in the vicinity are similar dedications. CIL. III. 1, 979; 980; 1079.

A freedman dedicates to A. with Jupiter, Juno and Minerva. CIL. Supp. III. 2, 7740.

Cibinium. Dedication to A. CIL. III. 1, 1614.

Galt. Dedications to A. and Hygieia. CIL. III. 1, 951; Supp. III. 2, 7720.

Mehadia. Dedications to A. and Hygieia; cure by water. CIL. III. 1, 1560; 1561.

Ulpia Trajana. Dedications to A.; to Hygieia; to A. Pergamenus and Hygieia. CIG. 6813. CIL. III. 1, 1417; 1417 a; 1427; Supp. III. 2, 7896-7898.

CHERSONESOS.

Coins: A. standing; Hygieia feeding serpent. Mionn. S II. 5, 23, 24.

THRACE.

Ainos. Coins: A. standing. Mionn. S II. 214, 58.

Bizye. Coins: A. seated with patera; Hygieia with Telesphoros; Hygieia feeding serpent. Mionn. I. 375, 78; S II. 233, 164, 169.

Byzantium. Coins: A. standing. Mionn. S II. 263, 378.

Deultum. Coins: A. standing; A. and Hygieia standing; Hygieia feeding serpent. Mionn. S. II. 277-300.

Hadrianopolis. Dedication to A. and Hygieia.
Coins: same types; Telesphoros. CIG. 2046.
Mionn. S II. 303-326; I. 375, 78.

Maroneia. Coins : A. standing.

Mionn. I. 393, 200 ; S II. 337, 830.

Mesembria. Coins : A. standing ; Hygieia feeding serpent.

Mionn. I. 394, 218 ; S II. 344, 860 ; 346, 874.

Odessos. Dedication to A.

CIG. 2056 F.

Coins : A. standing ; A. and Hygieia standing ; Hygieia feeding serpent.

Mionn. I. 397, 230 ; S II. 357, 927 ; 360, 942.

Pantalia. Coins : all of the above types ; A. reclining on a winged dragon; A. holding serpent-staff ; A. lying on coiled serpent.

Mionn. I. 398, 233 ; S II. 368–395.

Perinthos. Coins : A. standing ; A. and Hygieia standing.

Mionn. I. 409, 310 ; S II. 403–425.

Philippopolis. Coins : all the usual types.

Mionn. S II. 462–478.

Plotinopolis. Coins : A. standing ; Hygieia feeding serpent.

Mionn. S II. 480, 1638–1640 ; 481, 1646.

Serdika. Coins : usual types ; A. standing with a small naked figure raising the right hand.

Mionn. S II. 485–497.

Topiros. Coins : A. standing.

Mionn. S II. 502, 1759.

Trajanopolis. Coins : usual types of A., Hygieia and Telesphoros.

Mionn. I. 424, 383 ; S II. 512–515.

Hephaistia (an island of Thrace).   Coins : head of A.

Mionn. I. 432, 8.

MACEDONIA.

Amphipolis. Inscription set in sanctuary of A.

Ditt. 439.

Dium. Coins : A. standing.

Mionn. S. III. 64, 409.

Pera. Dedication to A. and Hygieia.

CIG. 2038.

PONTUS.

Amasea. Coins : A. and Hygieia.

B. M. Pontus, 9.

Amasos. Coins : A. and Hygieia.

B. M. Pontus, 22.

Kerasos. Coins : A. standing.

Mionn. S IV. 443, 157.

PAPHLAGONIA.

Aboniteichos (Ionopolis). Cult founded by imposture. Coins : A. and Hygieia standing.

Luc. Ἀλεξ. ἢ ψευδ.
Mionn. S IV. 550, 1.

Neoclaudiopolis. Coins : A. standing.

Mionn. S IV. 568, 104. Head, 433.

BITHYNIA.

Amastris. Coins: usual types of A. and Hygieia. Mionn. II. 390–395; S IV. 555–564.

Bithynium (Claudiopolis). Coins: A. standing; Hygieia feeding serpent. Mionn. II. 418, 49, 51; S V. 23, 118. Head, 437.

Caesareia-Germanica. Coins: A. with serpent. Head, 438.

Chalkedon. An inscription of uncertain origin giving evidence for the purchase of the priesthood and containing other matters relating to the cult has been referred to Chalkedon. Coll. 3052.

Hadrianus. Coins: bust of A. with Telesphoros; A., Hygieia and Telesphoros; A. and Hygieia. Mionn. II. 428–432; S V. 38–43.

Hadrianothera. Coins: A. standing. Mionn. II. 435; 138, 139.

Heraklea. Coins: A. standing; Hygieia feeding serpent. Mionn. II. 442, 169; S V. 61–67. B. M. Bith. 145.

Juliopolis. Coins: A. and Hygieia standing; Hygieia feeding serpent. Mionn. II. 446, 189; 448, 197; S V. 73–75. B. M. Bith. 150.

Kios. Coins: Hygieia feeding serpent. Mionn. II. 496, 463; S V. 250, 1463; 254, 1486. B. M. Bith. 136.

Nikaia. Coins: all the usual types; A. seated on winged serpent; altar with serpent and inscription ACKΛIΠIO; coins of the Asklepieia. Mionn. II. 452–463; S V. 89–151. Head, 443.

Nikomedia. Coins: A. standing; Hygieia feeding serpent. Mionn. II. 472, 336; S V. 181–209. B. M. Bith. 182 ff.

Prusa (ad Hypium). Coins: Hygieia feeding serpent. Mionn. II. 490, 431; S V. 244, 1430. B. M. Bith. 202.

Prusa (ad Olympum). Coins: A. standing; A., Hygieia and Telesphoros standing; Hygieia feeding serpent. Mionn. II. 480, 481; S V. 224–232. Head, 444.

Tium. Coins: A. standing; A. and Hygieia; Hygieia with serpent. Mionn. II. 500–502; S V. 260–269. B. M. Bith. 205 ff.

TROAS.

Abydos. Coins: staff of A. Mionn. II. 634, 27.

Alexandria Troas. Sanctuary of A. CIG. 3582.

Kelainai. Sanctuary mentioned. Strab. XIII. 1, 44.

AEOLIS.

Aigai. Coins: A. standing; A. and Hygieia. Mionn. III. 6, 24, 25.

Assos. Coins : A. at altar.

Head, 449.

Elaia. Mentioned by Aristides. .
Coins : usual types ; A. and Aphrodite.

Aristid. 486, 16.
Mionn. III. 15–21; S VI. 27–33.

Gargara. Coins : A. standing ; Telesphoros.

Mionn. II. 552, 249; S V. 358, 454. Head, 455.

Kame. Coins : Hygieia standing.

Head, 479.

Kyme. Coins : A. standing.

Mionn. III. 12, 72, 73.

Neontichos. Coins : Telesphoros.

Mionn. III. 24, 145.

Temnos. Coins : A. standing.

Mionn. III. 29, 172 ; S VI. 45, 46.

LESBOS.

Mytilene. The Asklepieion lay on the Acropolis of Mytilene. The priesthood was hereditary. Certain regulations in regard to the priests are found in inscriptions.
Dedications.
Decree set in temple.
Coins : usual types of A., Hygieia and Telesphoros; A. and Artemis standing with Kybele seated between.

Mitth. d. Arch. Inst. XIII. 56. Coll. 255 ; 260.

Mitth. d. Arch. Inst. XIII. 58, 74.
Mitth. d. Arch. Inst. XI. 263, l. 34.
Mionn. III. 44–59; S 66–77.

MYSIA.

Adramytion. Coins : A. standing.

Mionn. II. 516, 21.

Antandros. Coins : A. standing.

Mionn. II. 518, 29–31 ; S V. 287, 56.

Apollonia. Coins : A. standing; A., Hygieia and Telesphoros.

Mionn. II. 520, 42 ; S V. 290, 63.

Attaia. Coins : A. standing.

Head, 449.

Germe. Coins : A. standing ; Telesphoros.

Head, 455.

Kamena. Coins : A. standing.

Mionn. II. 526, 70.

Kyzikos. Coins : A. standing ; A., Hygieia and Telesphoros.

Mionn. II. 542, 194 ; S V. 319, 320. Head, 454.

Parion. Coins : A. *adolescens.* In front, a bull holding up his right foot on which A. is about to begin some operation ; Hygieia with patera.

Mionn. II. 578, 422 ; 584, 458 ; S V. 399–410.

Pergamon. The cult in Pergamon in the time of the Roman emperors was more important than in any other city. It was the centre of the worship, not only throughout Asia Minor, but in the regions west

of the Black Sea. The epithet Περγαμηνός, or Pergamenus, is frequently found in inscriptions.[1] The
hooded figure of Telesphoros is here most frequent
on coins.   His connection with Asklepios is of a
late date, and the origin is in Asia Minor, if not in
Pergamon itself, though similar personifications are
found in Sikyon and Epidauros.

The cult was said to be introduced from Epidauros
by Archias, son of Aristaichmos.[2]   The sanctuary of
the god lay at a little distance from the city,[3] as is
the case with most of those belonging to a crowded
town.   Aristides describes the location as most
wholesome, and the water supplies as beyond his
powers of expression.[4]

The ritual was suited to the character of the time
and place. It was unusually formal, public processions and sacrifices coming frequently during the
year. The Emperors were attracted to it, and took
part themselves in the elaborate ceremonial. Caracalla was treated here[5] and had many coins struck
showing himself in attitudes of adoration and sacrifice. The Asklepieia were celebrated here and with
great magnificence.[6] The sacrifice of bulls was made
to Asklepios here more than elsewhere, showing that
the public ritual was of more importance than the
private.[7] Prusias even went through the ceremony
of making an offering to the god before he plundered
the temple and carried off the statue.[8] The hero
Telephos was worshipped in the Asklepieion with
song[9] and sacrifice. But whoever partook of this
sacrifice must be purified before coming to the god
Asklepios.[10]

The Asklepieion was not only a temple and a cure-
establishment,[11] but a refuge, and as such was known
to Tacitus.[12]   Other allusions to the cult in Pergamon which, however, throw little light upon its
peculiarities are the following: Appian. de Bello
Mithr. 23; 60.   Julian. in Cyr. Alex. c. Jul. VI. 200.
Philost. Vit. Soph. 229; 266.   Stat. Silv. I. 4, 61 ff.;
III. 4, 6; 69, 80; III. pro. 25.

The coins from Pergamon show all the usual
types of Asklepios, Hygieia and Telesphoros, and
a number of new combinations are also seen. Perhaps the most peculiar are those coins representing
Asklepios in a chariot drawn by Centaurs which hold
torches in the hands. Asklepios sacrifices at an
altar before the Emperor, or the Emperor makes the

[1] Bau. Aus Epid. p. 14. CIG.
6753.   CIL. III. 1, 1417 a.

[2] Paus. II. 26, 8.

[3] "Pergamon" in BD. II.
1226.

[4] Aristid. 409, 9 ff.

[5] Herodian. IV. 8, 3.

[6] Mitth. d. Arch. Inst. XVI.
p. 132.

[7] CIG. 3538; Polyb. 32, 25, 1.
See coins.

[8] Polyb. loc. cit. and 4.   See
Suidas, art. Προυσίας.

[9] Paus. III. 26, 10.

[10] Paus. V. 13, 3.

[11] Luc. Ἰκαρομ. 24.
[12] Tac. Ann. III. 63.

offering. Jupiter, Diana, Nemesis, Nike, Demeter and Serapis all find place on the various Asklepios coins. The cult assumed a most cosmopolitan character, very different from its Greek form, but chiming in with the spirit of the age in which it found itself.[1]

W. Wroth. Ask. and the Coins of Pergamon. Mionn. II. 588 ff.; S V.; 442 ff. Head. 463 ff.

Pionia. Coins: A. standing.

Mionn. II. 625, 71. Head, 464.

Pitane. Coins: the Pentagon or Pentalpha was by the Pythagoreans called Hygieia according to Lucian. On coins it symbolizes the cult of Asklepios.

Head. 465.

Perperene. Coins: A. standing.

Mionn. II. 624, 706, 708; S V. 484, 1209.

Poimamenos. Famous temple of A.
Temple of A. and Apollo.
Coins: A. standing.

Aristid. 502, 21.
Mitth. d. Arch. Inst. IX. 32.
Mionn. II. 628, 725.

Porselene. Coins: A. standing; Telesphoros.

Mionn. II. 629, 731, 732; S V. 491, 492.

Stratonikeia (ad Caicum). Coins: A. standing.

Head, 466.

Thebe. Coins: A. standing; A. and Artemis with altar and serpent between; Telesphoros.

Mionn. S V 278, 282.

IONIA.

Apollonia. Coins: A. and Hygieia standing.

Mionn. III. 62, 7; S VI. 82, 9.

Ephesos. Coins: Artemis and A.

Mionn. S VI. 132-207.

Klazomenai. Coins: A. standing.

Mionn. III. 69-72; S VI. 91, 71.

Kolophon. Coins: A. with Apollo; A., Hygieia and Telesphoros.

Mionn. III. 78, 125, 127; S VI. 103, 149.

Magnesia. Coins: A. standing.

Mionn. III. 152, 668; 153, 670; S VI. 245, 1071.

Miletos. A. mentioned in Miletos.
Coins: A. and Apollo.

Theocrit. Ep. VII.
Mionn. III. 160, 786, 787; S VI. 275-280.

Phokaia. Coins: A. standing.

Mionn. III. 182, 866.

Smyrna. The cult came from Pergamon, and here the Asklepieion lay by the salt water.
Aristides makes frequent mention of this temple.
Dedications to A.; priest mentioned.
Coins: usual types of A., H. and Telesphoros; A. with Nemesis; Amazon holding statue of A.

Paus. II. 26, 9.

Aristid. 486, 16.
CIG. 3158; 3159; 3170. Cf. Kaibel 797.

CIG. 3052.

Teos. Stele placed in temple of A.
Coins: head of A.; A. standing; A. and Serapis.

Mionn. III. 260, 261; S VI. 382, 1038, 1039 Num. Zeitsch. 20, 117.

LYDIA.

Akrasos. Coins: A. standing; A. and Hygieia; A., Hygieia and Telesphoros.
Mionn. IV. 1, 2; 2, 9; S VII. 311-313. Head, 548.

Apollonis. Coins: A. and Hygieia standing.
Mionn. IV. 9, 48.

Attalia. Coins: A. standing; Telesphoros.
Mionn. IV. 12-14; S VII. 321, 42.

Daldis. Coins: usual types of A. and Hygieia.
Mionn. S VII. 342-345.

Dioshieron. Coins: A. standing; Hygieia.
Mionn. IV. 36-38. Head, 549.

Gordus-Julia. Coins: A. standing; Telesphoros.
Mionn. IV. 39, 202; 40, 206; S VII. 346, 137. Head, 549.

Herakleia. Coins: Hygieia feeding serpent.
Mionn. S VII. 349, 149.

Hermokapelia. Coins: A. standing.
Mionn. IV. 46, 243.

Hypaipa. Coins: A. standing; A. and Hygieia.
Mionn. IV. 51-57; S VII. 356-359.

Hyrkania. Coins: A. standing; Hygieia feeding serpent; Telesphoros.
Mionn. IV. 60-62; S VII. 364, 219, 220.

Kilbiani. Coins: A. and Hygieia; Telesphoros.
Mionn. IV. 31, 158; 32, 163; S VII. 337, 96, 99.

Maionia. Coins: Telesphoros.
Mionn. IV. 67, 357.

Magnesia. Coins: A. standing.
Mionn. IV. 70, 376.

Nakrasa. Coins: A. standing.
Mionn. IV. 95, 518.

Philadelphia. Coins: A. standing.
Mionn. S VII. 399, 376.

Saittenai. Coins: bust of A.; A. standing.
Mionn. IV. 110, 604; 111, 611.

Thyateira. Inscriptions from Thyateira mention two different temples of A. Festivals took place here, both the yearly one and τὰ μεγάλα Ἀσκληπίεια.
BCH. X. 415, 23, 24; XI. 463, 28; 476, 51.

   Coins: A. standing; A. and an Amazon with altar; A. and Pallas; A. and Apollo; A. and Dionysos; A. and Emperor Caracalla who sacrifices.
Mionn. IV. 157-166; S VII. 450, 615.

KARIA.

Antiochia. Coins: A. standing; A. and Hygieia.
Mionn. III. 318, 88; S VI. 449, 77.

Apollonia. Coins: A. standing; A. and Hygieia; Telesphoros.
Mionn. S VI. 473, 184; 475, 193. Head, 521.

Baiaca. Statues of A. and H. in temple of Zeus.
BCH. XII. 83, 9; 87, 11.

Bargasa. Coins: A. standing; A. and Hygieia; A., Hygieia and Telesphoros.
Mionn. III. 334, 183; 335, 188; S VI. 476, 195.

Bargylia. Coins: A. standing.
Mionn. III. 337, 198.

Chersonesos. Coins : Hygieia feeding serpent.   Mionn. II. 265, 50.

Euippe. Coins: Hygieia feeding serpent.   Mionn. III. 345, 249.

Halikarnassos. Coins; A. and Hygieia; A. and Apollo.   Mionn. III. 349, 267; S VI. 498–500.

Knidos. Dedication to A.   Coll. 3525, 3.
   Priest in Knidos.   Suid. art. Δημοκήδης.
   Coins : A. standing ; A. and Aphrodite.   Mionn. III. 343, 237, 239, 242.

Mylasa. Coins : A. standing; A. and Hygieia.   Mionn. III. 357–358; S VI. 511, 373.

Peraia (Phoinix). Priest of A. mentioned.   BCH. X. 249.

Pharasa. Coins : Staff of A.   Head, 530.

Stratonikeia. A. and Hygieia in connection with Zeus and other gods.   BCH. VII. p. 85, 88.
   Coins : A. and woman standing.   Mionn. III. 381, 457.

Trapezopolis. Coins : A. standing.   Mionn. III. 388, 489.

DORIAN ISLANDS.

Astypalaia. A stele is placed in the Hieron of A.   Coll. 3462.
   Dedication to A.; temple mentioned.   CIG. 2485; 2491. Cf. Paton and Hicks, Inscr. of Cos. p. 30.
   Coins: head of A.; serpent-staff.   Mionn. S VI. 563, 5.

Chalke. Dedication to A.   Ross. Inscr. Ined. II. 290.

Karpathos. Festival of A. mentioned.   Rev. Arch. 1863, p. 470, l. 23.

Kasos. Dedication to A.   Ross. Inscr. Ined. II. 260.

Kos. The island of Kos was celebrated as the starting point of the scientific study of medicine under Hippocrates in the fifth century. The story of his knowledge of the temple-lore is familiar.   Strab. VIII. 6; Pliny, N. H. 29, 2.

There are said to have been three temples in the island,[1] and the location of healing springs in the eastern part makes it probable that one stood there.[2] The main temple was without the city[3] and served as an asylum for refugees.[4]

[1] See Berl. Phil. Wochenschrift, 1887, p. 1554.
[2] Paton and Hicks, Inscr. of Cos, p. 137.
[3] Strab. XIV. 2, 20.
[4] Tac. Ann. IV. 14.

Other references to the cult are numerous. Dion. Cass. 51, 8; Herond. II. 97; IV. 2; Hdt. VII. 99; Paus. III. 23, 6; Tac. Ann. XII. 61; Paton and Hicks, Inscr. of Cos, Nos. 8; 10; 14; 30; 92; 103; 104; 130; 401; 402; 406; 408; BCH. V. p. 211, n. 6.

Coins : of no earlier than second century; usual types of A. and Hygieia; head of A. crowned with laurel or fillets.   Mionn. III. 401–411; S VI. 567–582.

Crete. In *Lebena*, now Leda, the eastern of the two harbor towns south of Gortyna, was a much frequented Asklepieion, to which came persons even from Libya.[1]

According to Pausanias, the cult was directly derived from Kyrene,[2] but more remotely it came from Arkadia, from which the worship of A. παῖς was transmitted.[3]

The priesthood appears to have been hereditary.[4] A cult-statue is mentioned.[5]

Two statues of Ὄνειρος offered to A.

Coins: A. standing; A. and Hygieia.

A treaty between Gortyna and Hierapytna was inscribed in set in the temple of A. This temple may be the one at Lebena, or a second at Hierapytna, which is nowhere else mentioned.

Coins: A. seated, with serpent, from *Priansos*, a town of Crete.

Rhodos. The Asklepieion and enclosure are mentioned.

Thera. The priesthood was here hereditary.

PHRYGIA.

Aizanis. Coins: A. standing; Hygieia feeding serpent.

Akmonia. Coins: A. standing; A. and Hygieia.

Ankyra. Coins: Hygieia feeding serpent; Telesphoros.

Attalia. Coins: A. standing; A. and Poseidon.

Attuda. Coins: A. standing; Hygieia feeding serpent; A., Hygieia and Telesphoros.

Bruzas. Coins: Asklepios; Hygieia.

Dionysopolis. Coins: Asklepios; Telesphoros.

Dokimaion. Coins: Asklepios.

Eukarpia. Coins: Telesphoros.

Grimenothyrae (Trajanopolis). Coins: A. standing; A. and Hygieia.

Hierapolis. Coins: head of A.

---

[1] Philost. Vit. Apoll. IV. 34, p. 79. Strab. X. 478.

[2] Paus. II. 26, 9.

[3] AZ. 1852, pl. 38.
[4] Philol. 1889, 401 ff.; 1890, 577 ff.
[5] Bau. Aus Epid. 6.
Kaibel, 839.
Mionn. II. 260, 18, 20; S IV. 301, 39, 40.
CIG. 2555.

Mionn. S IV. 339, 280.

Diodor. 19, 45; BCH. IV. 139.

Ross. Inscr. Ined. II. 221.

Mionn. IV. 205–212, S VII. 488–499.

Mionn. IV. 196–203; S VII. 484, 15.

Mionn. IV. 223, 171; S VII. 504, 112.

Mionn. IV. 239, 240; S VII. 515–518.

Mionn. IV. 242–246.

Head, 560.

Head, 562.

Mionn. IV. 283, 507. Head, 562.

Mionn. IV. 290, 547.

Head, 564.

Mionn. S VII. 567, 365.

Hieropolis. Coins: A. standing.	Mionn. IV. 306, 307. Head, 565.
Kadi. Coins: A., Hygieia and Telesphoros ; A. and Hygieia.	Mionn. IV. 252, 343 ; S VII. 528, 226 ; 530, 232.
Kibyra. Coins: A. standing ; A. and Hygieia.	Mionn. IV. 258, 378 ; 259, 382, 383.
Kidyessos. Coins: Asklepios ; Hygieia.	Head, 561.
Kolossai. Coins: similar types.	Head, 561.
Kotiaion. Coins: A. standing ; A., Hygieia and Telesphoros.	Mionn. IV. 274-279 ; VII. 546-550.
Lampsakos. Festival of A. held with elaborate ceremonial.	CIG. 3641 *b.*
Laodikeia. Coins: A. standing ; Hygieia feeding serpent ; Zeus and A. Festival of A. shown by inscription ΑΣΚΛΗΠΙΕΙΑ on one coin.	Mionn. IV. 323-331 ; S VII. 580, 422. Head, 566.
Midaion. Coins: A. standing.	Mionn. IV. 342, 850.
Nakolea. Coins: A. standing ; A. and Hygieia.	Mionn. S VII. 604, 530, 531.
Otrus. Coins: head of A.; Telesphoros.	Mionn. S VII. 604, 632. Head, 567.
Peltai. Coins: head of A.; A. standing ; Hygieia feeding serpent.	Mionn. IV. 348, 881.
Prymnessos. Coins: A. standing ; Serapis.	Num. Zeitsch. 21, 176.
Sala. Coins: A. and Hygieia ; A., Hygieia and Telesphoros.	Mionn. IV. 358-360.
Siblia. Coins : Telesphoros.	Mionn. S VII. 617, 578.
Stektorion. Coins: A. standing; Hygieia feeding serpent.	Mionn. IV. 361, 945, 947.
Synaos. Coins: A. standing ; A. and Hygieia ; Telesphoros.	Mionn. IV. 363, 954-956 Head, 569.
Synnada. Coins : A., Hygieia and Telesphoros.	Mionn. IV. 369, 993, 994.
Themisonion. Coins : A. and Hygieia.	Mionn. S VII. 626, 606.
Tiberiopolis. Coins: A. standing.	Mionn. S. VII. 628, 614.
Tripolis. Coins : Telesphoros.	Head, 570.

PISIDIA.

Antiochia. Coins: Hygieia with serpent.	Mionn. S VII. 91, 13.
Ariassos. Coins : A. standing.	Head, 590.

Lyrbe. Coins: A., Hygieia and Telesphoros.   Mionn. S VII. 118, 147.

Sagallos. Coins: A. standing.   Mionn. S VII. 125, 167.

Selge. Coins: Hygieia feeding serpent.   Mionn. III. 525, 192; S VII. 135, 211.

LYKIA.

Rhodiopolis. A. and Hygieia are found here together. Festivals of the god.   CIG. 4315 n.

PAMPHYLIA.

Attalia. Coins: A. standing; Pallas, Hygieia and Nemesis.   Mionn. III. 451, 36; S VII. 37, 55.

LYKAONIA.

Parläis. Coins: A. and Hygieia.   Head, 596.

KILIKIA.

Aigai. The cult in Aigai is mentioned by Philostratus,[1] and the temple and its destruction by ecclesiastical fathers.[2]
  Coins: usual types; A. and Telesphoros in temple, with dedication to both as gods; A. and Telesphoros with kid.   [1] Philost. Vit. Apoll. I. 7, p. 4 ff. [2] Euseb. Vit. Const. III. 56; Sozomen. Eccl. Hist. II. 5; Zonaras, XIII. 12 c. Mionn. III. 542-546; S VII. 155-166.

Argos. Coins: A. seated with serpent.   Mionn. S VII. 196, 192, 193.

Irenopolis. Coins: A. standing; Hygieia feeding serpent.   Head, 603. Mionn. III. 587, 235; S VII. 217-223.

Kolybrassos. Coins: Hygieia.   Head, 601.

Lyrbe. Coins: A. standing.   Head, 605.

Soli. Alexander sacrificed here to A. Festivals took place in honor of the god.   Arrian. Anab. II. 5, 8. Q. Curt. Rufus, Hist. Alex. III. 7, 3.

Syedra. Coins: A. standing.   Mionn. IV. 616, 374.

Tarsos. Coins: A., Hygieia and Telesphoros; A. and Herakles in temple.   Mionn. S VII. 276-284.

GALATIA.

Ankyra. The festivals of A. were of unusual importance. They are frequently mentioned in inscriptions,[3] and certain coins bear the words, ΑCΚΛΗΠΕΙΑ CΩΤΗΡΕΙΑ,[4] while one has a vase   [3] BCH. IX. 69; CIG. 3428; 4016; 4017. [4] Head, 629.

with a similar inscription, a representation of some
prize given at the games.[1]

   Dedication to Sol, A. and Hygieia.

   Coins: all the usual types.

Pessinus. Coins: A. standing; Hygieia feeding serpent.

Sebaste. Coins: A. standing.

Tanion. Coins: Hygieia feeding serpent.

[1] Mionn. IV. 385, 69.

CIL. III. 1, 242.

Mionn. IV. 379-389; S VII.
634-640.

Mionn. IV. 392-396; S VII.
646, 72.

Mionn. S VII. 649, 85.

Mionn. S VII. 652, 93.

KAPPADOKIA.

Kataonia. Dedications to Apollo and A.

Tyana. Coins: A., Hygieia and Telesphoros.

BCH. VII. 132, 8, 9, 10.

Mionn. IV. 441, 234.

ISLANDS OF THE AEGEAN SEA.

Aigina. Sanctuary mentioned.

Amorgos. From the town of *Aigia* come coins with
representations of cupping instruments. Does this
evidence for the existence of a cult of A. overbalance
the fact of there being no spring or stream?

   Coins of before 300 B.C. bearing the head of A.
have been found in Amorgos.

   Anchiale. Coins: A. standing; head of A.

Anaphe. Decree set in Hieron of A.

   Dedication to A.

Delos. Sanctuary of A. mentioned.

   A. is connected with gods of the Orient.

   Epithet Αυσάνιοs.

   Offerings to A. were placed in temple of Apollo.

Klaros. Temple mentioned.

Kythera. "Aus Palaeokastro stammt ein Fragment
eines Asklepiosreliefs."

Melos. Dedications.

Paros. Dedications to A. and Hygieia.

Pordoselene. Fines paid to A.

Samos. Dedication to A. and Hygieia.

Syros. Dedication as thank-offering after a shipwreck.

Arist. Vesp. 123.

BCH. I. 218.

Mionn. S VII. 188, 166. Head,
409. See Mitth. d. Arch.
Inst. I. 331.

Coll. 3430.

Coll. 3452.

CIG. 2292; 2953 B; Ditt.
367.
BCH. VI. 498, n. 16; VII.
366.
Mon. gr. 1878, n. 7, p. 45.
BCH. VI. 29 ff.

Aelian. X. 49.

Mitth. d. Arch. Inst. V. 232.

CIG. 2428; 2429 a and b.
CIG. 2390-2397. CIG. 2046;
BCH. I. 134, n. 42; 44-48.
'Αθήρ. V. n. 21; 22; 23;
24; 34.
Coll. 304 B.

Mitth. d. Arch. Inst. IX. 256.

BCH. II. 87.

PHOENICIA.

In Phoenicia Asklepios was thought to be similar to one of the native gods. His ancestry is not at all as in Greece. He takes on a more mystical character, as brother of the Kabeiri, and is identical with *Esmun.*

Philo. Bybl. Frag. 27. Damasc. Βίος Ἰσ. in Phot. Bibl. II. 352. Cf. Paus. VII. 23, 8.

Strabo tells of an Asklepieion in a grove between Berytos and Sidon.

Strab. XVI. 2, 22.

Tyre. Coins: Inscription ΑΣΚΛΗΠΕΙΑ.

Head, 676.

MEDIA.

Ekbatana. Temple destroyed by Alexander.

Arrian. Anab. VII. 14, 5.

SAMARIA.

Caesarea. Coins: A. standing.

Mionn. V. 492, 31.

JUDAEA.

Ascalon. A. mentioned.

Marin. Procl. 19.

EGYPT.

Alexandria. Asklepieion mentioned.
   Coins: bust of A.; of Hygieia; A. sacrificing at altar; A. and Demeter.

Aelian. H. A. XVI. 39.
Mionn. VI. 188–441; S IX. 80–117.

Memphis. Cult of A. mentioned.
   Tacitus identifies Asklepios with Osiris.

Ammian. Marcellin. 22, 14, 7.
Tac. Hist. IV. 84.

Philis. A small sanctuary of A. dedicated by Ptolemy Epiphanes, 205–151 B.C.

CIG. 4894.

Ptolemais. A temple consecrated by Trajan between 98 and 102 A.D. A pæan has recently been found very similar in form and content to the familiar ones from Athens.

Rev. Arch. 1889, p. 71 ff.

MAURETANIA.

Caesarea. Temple of A. dedicated.

CIL. VIII. 2, 9320.

NUMIDIA.

Calama. Dedication to A.

CIL. VIII. 1, 5288.

Lambaesis. Temple of A. and Hygieia; dedications.

CIL. VIII. 1, 2579–2590; 2624.

Ulpia Marciana Trajana. Altar to A.

CIL. VIII. 1, 2340.

AFRICA (in general).

Carthage. The temple stood on the summit of the Acropolis. — Appian. Lib. 130; Strab. XVII. 3, 14.

Chisidio. Altar dedicated to A. — CIL. VIII. 1, 1267.

Hammam Ellif. Dedication to A. — CIL. VIII. 1, 997.

Kyrene. There were at least two shrines in Kyrene; one in *Balagrai*, where A. came as a physician from Epidauros, and in Kyrene itself. — Paus. II. 26, 9. CIG. 5131. Tac. Ann. 14, 18.

Municipium Thibica. To A. Augustus. — CIL. VIII. 1, 765.

Thibursicum. Dedication to A. — CIL. VIII. 2, 10618.

Thignica. Dedication to A. — CIL. VIII. 1, 1413.

ITALY.

The following towns in Italy, where the cult of Aesculapius existed, are not the only ones. These have been gathered for the most part from the evidence of inscriptions and coins. Other material can be found in the Latin writers. It has, however, not been thought best to extend this work much beyond the Greek world, though much use has already been made of Latin sources. The cult in Italy was extended from Rome, while the Sicilian cult more probably came direct from Epidauros.

Aeclanum. Dedication to A. — IGS. et I. 689.

Amiternum. Dedication to A. — CIL. IX. 4512.

Atina. Altar dedicated to A. — CIL. X. 1, 330.

Asculum. Dedication to A. — CIL. IX. 660.

Auximum. Dedication to A. and Hygieia. — CIL. IX. 5823.

Bononia. Dedications. — CIG. 6737; 6738. IGS. et I. 2282; 2283.

Croton. Temple of A. — Iambl. Pythag. Vit. 126.

Etruria. Coins: head of A.; serpent. — Head, 14.

Grotta Ferrata (Latium). Dedication to A. — CIL. XIV. 2493.

Pompeii. Dedication to A. — IGS. et I. 968.

Praeneste. Dedication to Esculapius. — CIL. XIV. 2846.

Puteoli. Dedications to A. and Hygieia. — IGS. et I. 832; CIL. X. 1, 1546; 1547; 1571.

Rhegium. Coins : A. seated ; heads of A. and Hygieia.   Head, 95, 96.

Rome. On the occasion of a plague which broke out in the city in the year 292 B.C., the Romans were advised by the Delphian oracle to introduce the cult of Asklepios. Within a year, the god in serpent's shape was brought from Epidauros to Tiberina, an island lying near Rome.[1]

[1] Arnob. VII. 44. Augustin. de Civ. Dei, III. 12, 7 ; X. 16, 36. Livy, X. 47 ; XXIX. 11, 1 ; Epit. XI. Ovid, Met. XV. 660 ff. Pliny. N. H. 29, 72. Valer. Max. I. 8, 2.

A second temple stood in the city itself.[2]

[2] Plaut. Curc. I. 1, 14. Cf. Sueton. II. 59.

A number of inscriptions relate to this cult.[3]

[3] CIG. 5913; 5976; 5978; 5979; 5980. IGS. et I. 968; 1096; 1125; 2416₂; CIL. VI. 1, 1-20.

Tarentum. The cult is said to have come from Epidauros to Tarentum, and thence to Rome.   Julian in Cyr. Alex. c. Jul. VI. 200.

Tegianum. Dedication to A.   CIL. X. 1, 284.

SICILY.

Agrigentum. The temple of A. lay before the city.   Polyb. 1, 18, 2. Cf. Cic. Verr. IV. 57.
The festivals of A. are noticed on coins.   Mionn. I. 214, 53.
Coins : head of A.; A. standing.   Head, 108.

Menaenum. Coins : Asklepios with staff.   Head, 132.

Messana. Cult mentioned.   Polyaenus, V. 2, 19.
Dedication to A. and Hygieia.   IGS. et I. 402.

Selinus. Coins : Altar of A. with cock.   Head, 147.

Syracuse. The epithet Ἐπιδαύριος may indicate that the cult came directly from Epidauros.   Cic. de Nat. Deor. 3, 34, 83 ; Clem. Alex. protr. 4, 52.
The worship of A. here is mentioned by Athenaeus.   Athenae. VI. 250 c ; XV. 693 e.
Coins : head of A. with serpent.   Head, 165.

Paulus Gerreus. Dedication to A. in both Latin and Greek. The epithet *Marre* is Phoenician, and shows a connection of this cult with that of Carthage.   IGS. et I. 608. Cf. CIL. X. 2, 7856.

SARDINIA.

Cerales. Dedications to A.   CIL. X. 2, 7852 ; 7853 ; 7857 ; 7604.

GALLIA CISALPINA.

Aquileia. Dedications to A.; A. Augustus; A. and Hygieia.   CIL. V. 1, 726-731 ; V. 2, 8206, 8207.

Bellunum. Dedication to A. Augustus.   CIL. V. 1, 2036.

Libactium. Dedication to A.   CIL. V. 1, 2034.

Pola. Dedication to A.   CIL. V. 1, 6.

Taurini. Dedication to A. and Hygieia.   CIL. V. 2, 6970.

GALLIA NARBONENSIS.

Augustum. Dedication to A. Augustus.   CIL. XII. 2386.

Gratianopolis. Dedication to A.   CIL. XII. 2215.

Nemausus (?). Dedication to A.   CIL. XII. 3042.

Reii. Dedication to A. of a statue of Somnus, and   CIL. XII. 354.
surgical instruments.

HISPANIA.

Bracera Augusta. Dedication to A. and Hygieia.   CIL. II. 2411.

Caldas de Vizella. Dedication to a number of gods,   CIL. II. 2407.
among whom A. is mentioned.

Carthago Nova. Cult of A. mentioned.   Polyb. X. 10, 8.

Merobriga. Physician dedicates to A.   CIL. II. 21.

Nescania. Dedication to Apollo and A.   CIL. II. 2004.

Olisipo. Dedications to A. Augustus.   CIL. II. 173-175.

Saguntum. Dedication to A. Augustus.   CIL. II. 3819.

Valentia. Dedication to A.   CIL. II. 3725, 3726.

ENGLAND.

Dedications to Asklepios both in Latin and Greek.

Ellenborough.   I.G.I.B. 2551.

Lancaster.   I.G.I.B. 2552 ; CIL.VII. 431.

Chester. To A. and Hygieia.   CIL. VII. 164.

BIBLIOGRAPHY.

———•◦•———

Anderson, J. The Temple of Aesculapius. Brit. Med. Jour. (1887), II. p. 904 ff.

Bauer, A. Die griechischen Ausgrabungen in Epidauros. Ztschr. f. Allg. Gesch. (1886), III. p. 553 ff.

Baunack, Joh. Epigraphische Kleinigkeiten aus Griechenland. Philol. (1889) 48, p. 401 ff.

Baunack, Theod. Inschriften aus d. kretischen Asklepieion. Philol. (1890) 49, p. 577 ff.

Baunack, Joh. and Theod. Studien auf dem Gebiet d. gr. u. ar. Sprachen, I. 1. Aus Epidauros.

Blass, F. Der Pæan des Isyllos. Jahrb. f. Phil. u. Päd. (1885), p. 822 ff.

Curtius, E. Griechische Ausgrabungen. Nord u. Süd, April, 1877.

Defrasse, A. and Lechat, H. Notes sur Épidaure. BCH. 14 (1890), p. 631 ff.

Diels, H. Antike Heilwunder. Nord u. Süd, 44, p. 130 ff.

Dragumis. Ἡ ὑπὸ τὸ νότιον τεῖχος τῆς Ἀκροπόλεως ἀνασκαφή. BCH. I. p. 330 ff.

v. Duhn, F. Griechische Reliefs gefunden in den Ausgrabungen der arch. Gesellschaft am Südfuss der Akropolis vom April, 1876 bis Juni, 1877. Mit einem Anhang enthaltend die Beschreibung der Votivreliefs an Asklepios in den athenischen Sammlungen. AZ. 1877, p. 139 ff.

Dyer, L. The Gods in Greece, Ch. VI. (1891).

Eschweiler, A. Ueber den Namen und das Wesen des gr. Heilgottes. Programm d. Gymnas. zu Brühl. (1885).

Fabricius, E. Art. Pergamon in BD. II. 1226.

Foucart, P. Édifices d'Épidaure. BCH. 14, p. 589 ff.

Fowler, H. N. The Statue of Asklepios at Epidauros. Am. Jour. of Arch. (1887), III. 2.

Friedländer, L.   Darstell. aus d. Sittengesch. Roms. III. pp. 496 ff.; 536 ff.

Gaidoz, H.   Apropos des chiens d'Épidaure.   Rev. Arch. (1884), II. p. 217 ff.

Gauthier, A.   Recherches historiques sur l'exercice de la médecine dans les temples chez les peuples de l'antiquité.   Paris-Lyon, 844.

Girard, P.   Catalogue descriptif des exvoto à Esculape.   BCH. I. p. 156 ff.

—— Exvoto à Esculape.   BCH. II. p. 65 ff.

—— L'Asclépieion d'Athènes d'après de récentes découvertes. Paris, 1882.

    REVIEWS.   *Beurlier*.   Bull. crit., 1882, 15. Juin, p. 41.

        Haussouillier, B.   Rev. Arch., 1882, p. 247 ff.

        Heydemann. . Phil. Rundschau, 1882, p. 1276 ff.

        v. Trendelenburg.   Berl. Phil. Wochenschr., 1882, p. 1057 ff.

        v. Wilamowitz-Möllendorf.   Deutsch. Ltz., 1882, p. 1375 ff.

—— **and Martha, J.**   Inventaires de l'Asclépieion.   BCH. II. p. 419 ff.

Göll, H.   Heilige Kurorte im Altertum.   Ausland, 1885, 10, p. 191 ff.

Harrison, J.   Mythology and Monuments of Ancient Athens, p. 297 ff.   London, 1890.

Häser, H.   Geschichte der Medicin, I.^{3} p. 68 ff.   Jena, 1875.

Hoffmann, F.   Die Traumerdeutung in den Asklepien.   Zurich, 1884.

Köhler, U.   Der Südabhang der Akropolis von Athen.   Mitth. d. Arch. Inst. II. pp. 171 ff.; 229 ff.

Kumanudis, S.   In 'Αθήναιον, V and VI.

Lambert, M.   Plan des Fouilles par la Société archéologique sur le versant méridional de l'Acropole.   BCH. I. p. 169 ff.

Larfeld, W.   Heilinschriften.   Burs.-Müll. Jahresb. 52, p. 457 ff.

Loewe, A.   De Aesculapii Figura.   1887.

Lolling, H. G.   Topographie von Athen.   Müller's HB. III. 329, 2.

Magnus, H.   Kulturgeschichtliche Bilder aus d. Entwicklung des ärztlichen Standes.   Breslau, 1890.

Merriam, A. C.   The Treatment of Patients in the Temples of Aesculapius.   Boston Med. and Sur. Jour. 112, p. 304 ff.

—— Dogs of Asklepios.   Amer. Antiquary, 7, p. 285.

Merriam, A. C. Aesculapius as Revealed by Inscriptions. Gaillard's Med. Jour., May, 1885.

Milchhöfer, A. Asklepios. BD. I. p. 194 ff.

Nägelsbach, K. F. Nachhomerische Theologie. p. 171 ff.

Panofka, Th. Die Heilgötter der Griechen. Abhandl. d. Berl. Akad. d. Wissensch., 1843, p. 157 ff.

—— Asklepios u. die Asklepiadae. *id.*, 1845, p. 271 ff.

du Prel, C. Die Mystik der alten Griechen. Leipzig, 1888.

Puschmann, Th. Jahresb. über die Medicin bei den Griechen und Römern. Burs.-Müll. Jahresb. 64, p. 285 ff.

Reinach, S. La seconde stèle des guérisons miraculeuses, découverte à Épidaure. Rev. Arch., 1885, I. p. 265.

—— Chronique d'Orient, Épidaure. *id.*, 1884, II. p. 78.

—— Les chiens dans le culte d'Esculape et les *Kelabim* des stèles peintes de Citium. Rev. Arch., 1884, II. p. 129.

v. Rittershain, G. A. Der medicinische Wunderglaube und die Inkubation im Altertum. Berlin, 1878.

Robiou, F. Aesculapius. Dictionn. I. p. 124 ff.

Saglio, E. Asklepieion. Dictionn. I. p. 470 ff.

Stark, B. Epiphanien d. Asklepios u. ihre Darstellung durch die Kunst. AZ., 1851, p. 314 ff.

v. Sybel, L. Asklepios u. Alkon. Mitth. d. Arch. Inst. X. p. 97 ff.

Thraemer, E. Asklepios. Roscher, Lex. d. Myth.

Urlichs, H. L. Asklepios und die Eleusinischen Gottheiten. Jahrb. d. Ver. d. Altertümer im Rheinl. 1889.

Vercoutre, A. La médecine sacerdotale dans l'antiquité grecque. Rev. Arch. 1885, II. p. 273 ff.; 1886, I. pp. 22 ff., 106 ff.

Weil, R. Das Asklepieion von Naupaktos. Mitth. d. Arch. Inst. IV. p. 22 ff.

Welcker, F. G. Griechische Götterlehre. II. p. 732 ff.

—— Incubation. Kl. Schriften. III. p. 89 ff.

Wide, S. Lakonische Kulte. p. 182 ff. Leipzig, 1893.

v. Wilamowitz-Möllendorf, U. Hippys von Rhegion. Hermes XIX. p. 448 ff.

—— Die Wunderkuren des Asklepios von Epidauros. Philol. Wochenschr., 1884, p. 1010 ff.

v. Milamowitz-Möllendorf, U. Isyllos von Epidauros. Philol. Untersuch. (1886), IX.

—— Die Kuren von Apellas. *ibid.*

Wolters, P.   Darstellungen des Asklepios.   Mitth. d. Arch. Inst. XVII. p. 1 ff.

Wroth, W.   Asklepios and the Coins of Pergamon.   Num. Chron. III. 2, p. 1 ff.

—— Miracles of Asklepios.   Antiq. n. s. 10, 259.

—— A Statue of the Youthful Asklepios.   Jour. Hell. Stud. IV. p. 46 ff.

Zacher, K.   Zu den Heilkunden von Epidauros.   Hermes, XIX. p. 467 ff.

LIST OF ABBREVIATIONS.

A Z.   Archäologische Zeitung.   Berlin, 1843.

Bau.   Baunack, J., Inschriften aus dem Asklepieion zu Epidauros; Studien auf dem Gebiete des griechischen und der arischen Sprachen von J. and Th. Baunack. Vol. I. Leipzig, 1886.

BCH.   Bulletin de Correspondance Hellénique.   Athens, 1877.

B D.   Baumeister, A., Denkmäler des klassischen Alterthums.   3 vols.   Munich, 1884–88.

B M.   Catalogue of Greek Coins in the British Museum, by R. S. Poole, B. V. Head, P. Gardner, W. Wroth.   London, 1873–88.

C I A.   Corpus Inscriptionum Atticarum consilio et auctoritate academiae regiae litterarum Borussicae editum.   Berlin, 1873.

C I G.   Corpus Inscriptionum Graecarum ed. A. Boeckh.   4 vols.   Berlin, 1825–77.

C I L.   Corpus Inscriptionum Latinarum consilio et auctoritate academiae litterarum regiae Borussicae editum.   Berlin, 1863.

Coll.   Sammlung der griechischen Dialektinschriften, herausgegeben von Dr. H. Collitz [und Dr. F. Bechtel].   Göttingen, 1884.

Ditt.   Dittenberger, W., Sylloge Inscriptionum Graecarum.   2 vols.   Leipzig, 1883.

H B.   Handbuch der klassischen Altertums-Wissenschaft in systematischer Darstellung herausgegeben von Dr. Iwan von Müller.   9 vols.   Munich, 1885–.

I G A.   Inscriptiones Graecae Antiquissimae praeter Atticas in Attica repertas consilio et auctoritate academiae litterarum regiae Borussicae ed. H. Roehl.   Berlin, 1882.

I G G S.   Corpus Inscriptionum Graecarum Graeciae Septentrionalis.   Vol. I ; ed. W. Dittenberger.   Berlin, 1892.

INDEX OF NAMES AND TOPICS.